Learn & Use

Microsoft® Excel®
in Your Classroom

Color CD included

- Technology Skills Lessons
- Leveled Content-Area Activities
- Project-Based Learning Activities

Author

Lynn Van Gorp, M.S.Ed.

SHELL EDUCATION

Publishing Credits

Contributing Authors
Erin K. Head
Eric LeMoine, M.Ed

Editor
Christine Dugan, M.A.Ed.

Assistant Editor
Torrey Maloof

Editorial Director
Emily R. Smith, M.A.Ed.

Editor-in-Chief
Sharon Coan, M.S.Ed.

Editorial Manager
Gisela Lee, M.A.

Creative Director
Lee Aucoin

Illustration Manager
Timothy J. Bradley

Print Production
Robin Erickson
Don Tran

Publisher
Corinne Burton, M.A.Ed.

Content Standards

Copyright 2004 McREL. www.mcrel.org/standards-benchmarks.

Shell Education

5301 Oceanus Drive
Huntington Beach, CA 92649-1030
http://www.shelleducation.com
ISBN 978–1–4258–0019–2
© 2007 Shell Education

Table of Contents

What Research Says About Technology Use in the Classroom

In recent years, technology use in the classroom has become widespread at all grade levels. In fact, a recent study by the U.S. Department of Education found that 75 percent or more of America's students were in schools with access to computers in classrooms or in labs (Mitchell, Bakia, and Yang 2007). Educators face the challenge of preparing students for a world that is becoming more technologically advanced with each passing moment. Therefore, students must learn how to use different forms of technology in the classroom and schools must equip their students with the skills and knowledge required to succeed in such an ever-changing world.

Technology use must be taught within an appropriate context—students should be able to make a connection between learning about a particular topic and knowing how technology can contribute to that learning experience. Therefore, integrating technology into content-area instruction is a key component to any effective technology program. Simply memorizing the steps needed to complete skills in isolation will not help students see the critical role that technology can play in learning about the real world. *Learn & Use Microsoft Excel in Your Classroom* offers a complete and integrated program—it takes practical and necessary technology skills and introduces them to students within the meaningful context of subject-matter content.

An extensive amount of research has been conducted over the years to determine how important and effective technology instruction is for student performance and achievement. Instructional technology, which includes computers, has been attributed to positive gains such as:

- increasing student achievement
- improving higher-order thinking skills and problem-solving abilities
- enhancing student motivation and engagement
- improving students' abilities to work collaboratively (White, Ringstaff, and Kelley 2002)

Gilbert Valdez, et al. (1999) also found similar signs of improvement, some of which extend beyond student learning. Their research finds that technology can:

- make learning more interactive
- enhance the enjoyment of learning
- individualize the curriculum to match the learners' developmental needs and interests
- capture and store data for informing data-driven decision making
- enhance avenues for collaboration among family members and the school community
- improve methods of accountability and reporting

These benefits highlight the importance of incorporating technology instruction into students' daily lives. However, many educators continue to struggle with finding the time to fully integrate technology. First, teachers have difficulty fitting technology training into their busy schedules. Then, if they do take a class, there is little time to practice what they've learned. Finally, without follow up and further training, important knowledge is lost (Mitchell, Bakia, and Yang 2007). This book helps teachers start integrating technology because it introduces the technology through commonly taught content-area topics.

What Research Says About Technology Use in the Classroom (*cont.*)

Michael Eisenberg and Doug Johnson (1996) argue that "effective integration of information skills has two requirements: 1) the skills must directly relate to the content-area curriculum and to classroom assignments and 2) the skills themselves need to be tied together in a logical and systematic information process model." Therefore, the organization and structure of *Learn & Use Microsoft Excel in Your Classroom* will help your students acquire proficiency with both subject-matter content and technology skills. Because the technology skills introduced in this book are organized in a logical and sequential order, students may build on their mastery of each skill as they progress through the lessons and activities. In addition, all skills are taught using topics that are directly related to content-area curriculum, and the lessons themselves are easily modified to fit the unique needs of your classroom curriculum.

The last part of this book focuses on project-based learning and technology. Project-based learning provides an "exciting balance between traditional teaching and technology tools" (Britt, Brasher, and Davenport 2007). The problem-based learning section also provides integrated lesson plans and activities. These activities, however, are more broad and open-ended, allowing students to enhance both their problem-solving abilities and their critical-thinking skills as they navigate their own ways toward producing final products. Students learn that using technology can provide them with a variety of choices as they make decisions about their own learning.

Microsoft Excel Skills

The lessons in this book are all written for use with *Microsoft Excel®* software. *Excel* is a spreadsheet program in which you can add data and create charts, reports, and other forms of graphic representations. *Excel* also allows users to create formulas and functions to perform mathematical calculations. Students can add color and other formatting to make their data more visually appealing to an audience. This exciting program provides a motivating and interesting way to input and organize data.

Learn & Use Microsoft Excel in Your Classroom will help guide you through the process of teaching students to use technology in appropriate, meaningful, and engaging ways. It will show students that *Excel* can be a powerful tool to help them learn about various topics and concepts and that technology can play a significant role in their development as learners.

The 36 lessons in this book are organized into 12 different technology skills. Each of the 12 skills listed on the following page is the main focus for three lessons, one for each grade span K–2, 3–5, and 6–8. Although a single technology skill is emphasized while teaching a lesson, other technology skills are presented and integrated in the activities themselves. Therefore, students who complete these activities have multiple opportunities to learn and practice various skills using *Excel* software.

Microsoft Excel Skills (cont.)

The technology skills included in this book may be introduced in different ways at different grade levels. Likewise, students in different grade levels may learn and use the same skill at slightly varying degrees of complexity. It is strongly recommended that you review all the lessons (even ones that are not written for the grade(s) you teach) for a particular skill to see which lesson may be the best fit for your students.

Twelve Technology Skills in This Book

- Getting Started
- Formatting Cells
- Changing Rows and Columns
- Sorting Lists
- Creating a Data Table
- Creating a Chart
- Working with Numbers
- Creating a Line Chart
- Creating a Pie Chart
- Using Functions and Formulas
- Displaying and Printing
- Special Features

How to Use This Book

Learn & Use Microsoft Excel in Your Classroom is divided into two sections. The first section of the book focuses on skill-based lesson plans. There are 36 lesson plans grouped under 12 different technology skills, ranging from easy to complex. For each technology skill, three different sample lessons are given.

Each technology skill is explained with a one-page summary. Screenshots are included with the list of steps to offer support as you learn the new technology skill before teaching it to your students. The screenshots shown in the book were taken using a Windows operating system. The summary pages with Macintosh screenshots are available on the Teacher Resource CD. (See page 207 for a list of filenames.) Keep in mind that there are often several ways to complete a single skill in *Excel*. Use the *Excel* Help menu, as necessary, to clarify any technology steps.

How to Use This Book (cont.)

In the second section of this book, the topic of using project-based learning strategies (PBL) with technology is explored and practical classroom applications are included. Four activities incorporate project-based learning techniques and have students creating projects using *Excel*. These projects differ from the earlier skill-based lessons in that they will likely take longer to complete, are more open-ended, and require that students work through the activities collaboratively with their peers. The activities are written in such a way that they can be used with broad themes and topics of study that reflect a truly authentic PBL experience.

Technology/Content Integration

While the lessons and projects in this book are designed to teach technology skills, the technology skills are integrated with subject matter from the four content areas: language arts, mathematics, science, and social studies. This makes the learning experience more authentic for students as they are using real software applications in meaningful and realistic ways. In addition, these teaching ideas give educators a way to motivate students by making core content more interesting and by making technology more applicable to real-world topics.

As you browse the core content topics that are included in this book, keep in mind that most of these lesson plans can be modified or altered to better fit the content that you are currently teaching. For example, a lesson on symmetry can be modified to address another mathematical topic. Likewise, a K–2 lesson on animals could be modified to teach about a more appropriate science topic for grades 6–8. Be creative and think about how the technology skills can be taught with the topics and units of study that you are currently teaching.

Lesson Plans

The lesson plans in this book include all the information that you need to prepare for instruction. Necessary materials are listed and suggestions for teacher preparation are described. Because the technology lessons in the book are also integrated with content-area material, some additional teaching may be required to introduce or review related content with students.

Once you are ready to begin working with *Excel*, a suggested procedure for teaching the lesson is listed sequentially. At the end of each lesson is a suggestion for extending the lesson for students who are ready to reach further within the content or technology skills.

The lesson plans specifically mention showing students samples for how to complete the various activities or projects. Student samples for all lessons and projects can be found on the Teacher Resource CD. (See page 206 for a list of sample project filenames.)

A list of steps, called Student Directions, is included for each lesson. This page can be projected for the whole class or can be distributed to students. This page lists what students will do once they are in front of the computers.

How to Use This Book (cont.)

Lesson Plans (cont.)

Although students will likely have seen the lesson modeled by you before approaching the computers on their own, the Student Directions serve as a reminder for students about what to do to complete the activity.

For project-based activities in which students have a great deal of choice about how to complete a project, the Student Directions page is a resource that may or may not fit with the ultimate direction of each student's project. Each project-based learning activity also includes a graphic organizer that is used at some point during the activity. This graphic organizer can be printed and copied for students to record information that will be used later in the activity.

One popular method of assessing student performance is using a rubric. A rubric is a tool that allows for standardized assessment of student work using specific criteria and a point grading scale. Rubrics are included for all lessons and projects in this book. They include space for both the teacher and the student to assess completed work. There is also a blank rubric file on the Teacher Resource CD (filename: *rubric.doc*). This may be used for either the skill lessons or project-based learning activities. When a project is assessed by both teacher and student, it allows students to be involved in the evaluation process of their own work and makes expectations clear.

Software Versions and Operating Systems

Most technology users know that a particular software is not always used in the exact same way by all users. This is true for *Excel* as well. Newer versions of the *Excel* program are released to reflect new updates and additional features. Likewise, *Excel* operates in different ways depending on whether it performs on either a Windows or Macintosh operating system.

In this book, every effort has been made to create lessons and student steps that can be completed regardless of your *Excel* version or your operating system. If a lesson's procedure or student steps do not appear to work on your computer or with your version of *Excel*, refer to the program's Help menu for further assistance.

Teacher Resource CD

A Teacher Resource CD accompanies the *Learn & Use Microsoft Excel in Your Classroom* book and includes supplementary materials that may be useful in your teaching. Student samples from each lesson, graphic organizers/data collection grids, summary pages with Macintosh screenshots, and a blank rubric are all included. See pages 206–207 for further information.

How to Use This Book (cont.)

Components of the Program

Introduction

- Concise overview of effective use of technology in the classroom
- Brief introduction to software and the 12 featured skills
- Description of how to best utilize this product in the classroom
- Correlation to standards

Summary Pages

- Brief description of new skill(s) being introduced
- Detailed step-by-step instructions of new skill(s)
- Multiple Windows screenshots to help guide instruction and offer support (Macintosh screenshots provided on Teacher Resource CD)
- Quick Tip provides shortcut or alternate way of using application

Procedure Sections

- Brief description of content-based lesson including content standard and technology skills
- Materials list
- Suggestions for teacher preparation
- Detailed step-by-step sequential instructions for teaching the lesson
- Extension ideas for differentiation

Student Directions

- List of steps for students to use while at the computers
- Help students complete the activity with little or no guidance

Rubrics

- Allow for standardized assessment of student work using specific criteria and a point grading scale
- Include space for both teacher and student to assess completed work
- Blank rubric on the Teacher Resource CD

How to Use This Book (cont.)

Components of the Program (cont.)

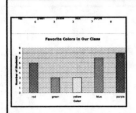

Student Samples

- Provide examples of what each project will look like when completed
- To be distributed or projected during the lesson to provide students with further instruction and guidance

Project-Based Learning Introduction

- Brief introduction to the project-based learning approach
- Explanation of how project-based learning fits with technology and integrates different subject areas and standards
- Description of how assessment is a critical piece of this learning process

Project-Based Learning Activities

- Allow students to apply everything they have learned throughout the book to real-life project-based activities
- Lessons include: activity description, content standard, technology skills, materials list, suggested teacher preparation, detailed procedure steps, and extension ideas for differentiation.

Graphic Organizers

- Included with each project-based learning activity
- Allow students to organize text and data before entering it into *Excel* worksheets

Appendices

- Works Cited and Other References
- Content-Area Index
- Teacher Resource CD Index
- Learn & Use Series Description

Teacher Resource CD

- Student Samples
- Graphic Organizers
- Data Collection Grids
- Mac Screenshots
- Blank Rubric

Correlation to Standards

The No Child Left Behind (NCLB) legislation mandates that all states adopt academic standards that identify the skills students will learn in kindergarten through grade 12. While many states had already adopted academic standards prior to NCLB, the legislation set requirements to ensure the standards were detailed and comprehensive.

Standards are designed to focus instruction and guide adoption of curricula. Standards are statements that describe the criteria necessary for students to meet specific academic goals. They define the knowledge, skills, and content students should acquire at each level. Standards are also used to develop standardized tests to evaluate students' academic progress.

In many states today, teachers are required to demonstrate how their lessons meet state standards. State standards are used in the development of Shell Education products, so educators can be assured that this product meets strict academic requirements.

How to Find Your State Correlations

Shell Education is committed to producing educational materials that are research and standards based. In this effort, all products are correlated to the academic standards of the 50 states, the District of Columbia, and the Department of Defense Dependent Schools. A correlation report customized for your state can be printed directly from the Shell Education website: **http://www.shelleducation.com**. If you require assistance in printing correlation reports, please contact Customer Service at 1-800-877-3450.

McREL Compendium

Shell Education uses the Mid-continent Research for Education and Learning (McREL) Compendium to create standards correlations. Each year, McREL analyzes state standards and revises the compendium. By following this procedure, they are able to produce a general compilation of national standards. Each lesson in this book is based on one or more of the McREL content standards. The chart on the next two pages lists the McREL standards that correlate to each lesson used in the book.

Correlation to Standards (cont.)

Lesson Title	Page Number	Content Area	Content Standard	Technology Skill
Number Fun	15	Mathematics	Students recognize written numerals.	Students open and save a new workbook and fill cells with colors.
Symmetry Design	19	Mathematics	Students understand the concept of symmetry.	Students open and save a new workbook and fill cells with colors.
Mystery Fill Design	23	Mathematics	Students understand the concept of geometric constructions.	Students open and save a new workbook and fill cells with colors.
Spelling Fun	28	Language Arts	Students use other resources to spell words.	Students format cells in worksheets.
Guess the Word	32	Language Arts	Students understand reading vocabulary.	Students format cells in worksheets.
Crossword Puzzle	36	Language Arts	Students use graphic representations to organize information and ideas.	Students format cells in worksheets.
Favorite Animal	41	Science	Students know that differences exist among individuals of the same kind of animals.	Students will change rows and columns in worksheets.
Cloud Information Chart	45	Science	Students know that water exists in the air in different forms.	Students will change rows and columns in worksheets.
Planet Comparison Chart	49	Science	Students know the characteristics of the eight planets in our solar system.	Students will change rows and columns in worksheets.
Reading List	54	Language Arts	Students read fiction appropriate to grades K–2.	Students know how to sort lists in a workbook application.
Book List	58	Language Arts	Students know the defining features of a picture book.	Students know how to sort lists in a workbook application.
Literature Record	62	Language Arts	Students read fiction appropriate to grades 6–8.	Students know how to sort lists in a workbook application.
Favorite Ice Cream Survey	67	Mathematics	Students understand that information about objects or events can be collected.	Students create data tables in a workbook application.
Favorite Pizza Survey	71	Mathematics	Students understand that data can be organized in many ways.	Students create data tables in a workbook application.
Favorite Elective Survey	75	Social Studies	Students interpret data in tables.	Students create data tables in a workbook application.
Favorite Ice Cream Chart	80	Mathematics	Students understand that information can be represented in graphs.	Students create charts in a workbook application.
Favorite Pizza Chart	84	Mathematics	Students construct bar graphs using data.	Students create charts in a workbook application.
Favorite Elective Chart	88	Mathematics	Students interpret data in tables.	Students create charts in a workbook application.
Helper Reward Chart	93	Mathematics	Students know that a number represents how many of something there is.	Students enter and work with numbers in a workbook application.
Weekend Schedule	97	Mathematics	Students understand that mathematical concepts can be represented symbolically.	Students enter and work with numbers in a workbook application.
Income and Expense Chart	101	Mathematics	Students add rational numbers.	Students enter and work with numbers in a workbook application.
Spelling Test Record	106	Language Arts	Students use letter-sound relationships to spell words.	Students use a workbook application to create line charts.

Correlation to Standards (*cont.*)

Lesson Title	Page Number	Content Area	Content Standard	Technology Skill
Temperature Averages Record	110	Science	Students know that water changes from one state to another through various processes.	Students use a workbook application to create line charts.
Stock Prices Record	114	Social Studies	Students know various types of specialized economic institutions found in market economies.	Students use a workbook application to create line charts.
Shoe Choice Chart	119	Mathematics	Students understand that information about objects or events can be collected.	Students use a workbook application to create pie charts.
Recess Activity Chart	123	Mathematics	Students understand that data can be organized in many ways.	Students use a workbook application to create pie charts.
Food Nutrition Chart	127	Science	Students know that making healthy food choices can be useful in attaining personal health goals.	Students use a workbook application to create pie charts.
Beginning Word Problems	132	Mathematics	Students add whole numbers.	Students use functions and formulas.
Intermediate Word Problems	136	Mathematics	Students multiply whole numbers.	Students use functions and formulas.
Advanced Word Problems	140	Mathematics	Students use computers for computation.	Students use functions and formulas.
Dinosaur Facts	145	Science	Students know that dinosaurs no longer exist.	Students know how to use different display and printing options in a workbook application.
Roller Coaster Facts	149	Science	Students know that when a force is applied to an object, the object might speed up.	Students know how to use different display and printing options in a workbook application.
Country Comparisons	153	Social Studies	Students know regions within continents.	Students know how to use different display and printing options in a workbook application.
Family Celebrations	158	Social Studies	Students understand family heritage through celebrations.	Students work with multiple worksheets and add headers and footers to their work.
City Population Statistics	162	Social Studies	Students know that the population of a city is the number of people who live in that city.	Students work with multiple worksheets and add headers and footers to their work.
Persuading an Audience	166	Social Studies	Students address reader counterarguments.	Students work with multiple worksheets, freeze panes, and add headers and footers to their work.
Surveying Favorites	176	Mathematics	Students understand that information can be represented in graphs.	Students use multiple skills to complete a project.
Lemonade Stand	182	Mathematics	Students determine reasonableness of a problem solution.	Students use multiple skills to complete a project.
Magic Squares	189	Mathematics	Students use trial and error to solve problems.	Students use multiple skills to complete a project.
Your Monthly Budget	196	Mathematics	Students use computers for computation.	Students use multiple skills to complete a project.

A *Microsoft Excel* worksheet (or spreadsheet) is a large grid made up of cells in rows (horizontal) and columns (vertical). Each cell has a location name based on the letter of the column and the number of the row in which it is located. For example, the first cell of a worksheet in the uppermost left column is referred to as cell A1 because it is located in Column A and in Row 1.

When first getting started with a *Microsoft Excel* worksheet, it is helpful to know how to open and save a file. Learning how to fill a cell with color is also important in organizing and highlighting data.

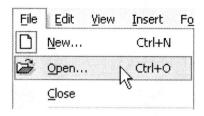

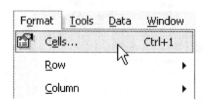

Quick Tip

To use any toolbar, click **View** on the Menu bar. Click **Toolbars>**. Choose a toolbar from the list. The *Standard* and *Formatting* toolbars are the most commonly used toolbars.

Step-by-Step Directions

Opening a New Excel File (Workbook)

1. Open *Microsoft Excel* and a new workbook will open. If a Project Gallery—New dialog box appears, click on the **Excel Workbook** icon and click **Open**.

2. If you are already working within *Microsoft Excel*, click **File** on the Menu bar. Click **New…** You may also click the **New** button on the *Standard* toolbar.

Opening a Saved Excel File (Workbook)

1. Click **File** on the Menu bar. Click **Open…** You may also click the **Open** button on the *Standard* toolbar.

2. In the dialog box, navigate to the folder where you saved your workbook.

3. Click the filename to select it. Click **Open**.

Filling Cells with Color

1. Select the cell or cells you wish to fill with color.

2. Click **Format** on the Menu bar. Click **Cells…** Select the *Patterns* tab on the Format Cells dialog box. Choose a color and click **OK**. You may also use the **Fill Color** button on the *Formatting* toolbar.

3. To select a different color using the **Fill Color** button on the *Formatting* toolbar, click the arrow just to the right of the **Fill Color** button. Click on a new color from the palette.

Number Fun

Lesson Description

Students open and save workbooks. They locate cells and work with filling cells with color.

Content Standard

Students recognize written numerals.

Technology Skill

Students open and save a new workbook and fill cells with color.

Additional Technology Skills

● using the Menu bar and toolbars

Materials

● student sample (filename: *fun.xls*)

Teacher Preparation

1. Print and review the student sample (filename: *fun.xls*).

2. You may want students to work independently, in pairs, or in small groups. You may even complete this lesson as a whole-class lesson. Review the procedure and consider various groupings before you begin to teach the lesson.

Procedure

1. Explain to the students that they will be learning how to get started using a workbook application. Open *Microsoft Excel*.

2. Open a workbook (or spreadsheet file) and show students that a worksheet (or spreadsheet) has boxes called *cells*. Share examples of the types of things they will learn how to do with this application.

3. Model for students how to open and save a workbook. (See page 14.) Emphasize to students that they should save their work often. Discuss how you would like them to name their projects. You may want students to use their names as part of their filenames.

4. Have students open and save their own workbook files.

5. Explain how each cell has a label that has a letter and a number. Highlight different cells and show students how they can tell what a cell's label is. Stress that columns are labeled with letters and rows are labeled with numbers. For example, the cell in Column A and Row 2 is known as A2.

Procedure *(cont.)*

6. Play a game in which students find specific cells. Call out a particular cell label and have students find the cell's location. Have them check the cell label in the top left corner of their worksheets to make sure their choice is correct. Make sure that the **Formula Bar** is selected so that students are able to see the cell labels. To do this, click **View** on the Menu bar and choose **Formula Bar**. Continue this game until students are able to find particular cells with ease.

7. Show students how to fill a cell with color. (See page 14.) Stress to students that they need to select the cell first before clicking **Format** on the Menu bar or the **Fill Color** button on the *Formatting* toolbar.

8. Have students add color to cells.

9. Show students how they can also change the color by using the arrow just to the right of the **Fill Color** button on the *Formatting* toolbar. (See page 14.)

10. Play a game in which students find specific cells and fill them with specific colors. Have the final product represent a number or a pattern. You may want to use the student sample (filename: *fun.xls*) provided on the Teacher Resource CD. You may either give students printed copies of the design and have them replicate it, or you may call out cell labels and colors and have students follow your directions.

11. Students do not need to print their worksheets at this time. This lesson's focus is on understanding how to setup a worksheet. You may want your students to print their projects later.

12. Have students share their work with you and their classmates.

13. Use the rubric provided on page 18 to assess this lesson.

Extension Ideas

Have students fill cells to represent number parts in word problem solutions. Example: If Susan bought 3 oranges and 5 apples at the store, how many pieces of fruit would she have in all? Students could color 3 orange squares and 5 red squares, for a total of 8 squares in all $(3 + 5 = 8)$.

Have students create designs by following specific guidelines. For example, you may give students a quantity for each cell color, such as 10 red, 6 blue, 4 green, and 1 yellow.

Student Directions

1. Open a new workbook.

2. Listen to your teacher's directions to create a design.

3. Click **Format** on the Menu bar.

4. Click *Cells*...

5. Click on the *Patterns* tab on the Format Cells dialog box.

6. Choose the correct color. Click **OK**.

7. Now, try using the **Fill Color** button on the *Formatting* toolbar to choose the next color.

8. Click **View** on the Menu bar.

9. Click *Toolbars>*.

10. Choose *Formatting*.

11. Listen to your teacher's directions to finish your design.

12. Save your work.

13. Share your work with others.

Assessment Rubric

Strong **(3 Points)**	The student filled all cells in the exact location required and with the correct colors.	The student correctly opened and saved a workbook.	The student was able to complete his or her work independently.	The student fully understands the lesson objectives.
Effective **(2 Points)**	The student filled three or four cell groups in the exact location required and with the correct colors.	The student opened and saved a workbook.	The student was able to complete his or her work with very little support.	The student mostly understands the lesson objectives.
Emerging **(1 Point)**	The student filled one or two cell groups in the exact location required and with the correct colors.	The student attempted to open and save a workbook.	The student was able to complete his or her work with support.	The student somewhat understands the lesson objectives.
Not Yet **(0 Points)**	The student was unable to fill the cells.	The student did not open and save a workbook.	The student was unable to complete his or her work.	The student does not understand the lesson objectives.
Self Score				
Teacher Score				
Total Score				

Comments:

Symmetry Design

Lesson Description

Students make symmetrical designs by locating and coloring worksheet cells.

Content Standard

Students understand the concept of symmetry.

Technology Skill

Students open and save a new workbook and fill cells with color.

Additional Technology Skills

- using the Menu bar and toolbars
- printing work

Materials

- visual examples of symmetry
- student sample (filename: *symm.xls*)

Teacher Preparation

1. Print and review the student sample (filename: *symm.xls*).

2. Create additional project samples for students to use as extra credit or challenge activities. These can be subject or theme related.

Procedure

1. Explain to students that they will be learning how to get started using the workbook application. Open *Microsoft Excel*.

2. Open a workbook (or spreadsheet file) and show students that a worksheet has boxes called *cells*. Share examples of the types of things they will learn how to do with this application.

3. Show students how to open and save new workbooks. (See page 14.) Emphasize to students that they should save their work often. Discuss how you would like them to name their projects. You may want students to use their names as part of their filenames.

4. Have students open and save their own workbook files.

5. Explain how each cell has a label that has a letter and a number. Highlight different cells and show students how they can tell what a cell's label is. Stress that columns have letter labels and rows have number labels. For example, a cell in Column A and Row 2 is known as A2.

Procedure *(cont.)*

6. Have students find different cells. Call out a particular cell label and have students find the cell's location. Have them check the cell label in the top left corner of their worksheets to make sure their choice is correct. Make sure that the **Formula Bar** is selected so that students can see the cell labels. To do this, click **View** on the Menu bar and choose **Formula Bar**. Continue until the students are able to find particular cells with ease.

7. Show students how to fill a cell with color. (See page 14.) Stress to students that they need to select the cell first before clicking **Format** on the Menu bar or the **Fill Color** button on the *Formatting* toolbar.

8. Show students how they can change the fill color by clicking on the arrow just to the right of the **Fill Color** button.

9. Tell students that they are going to make a symmetrical design using the Fill Color feature. Review the definition of *symmetry*. Explain to students that they can make their own designs or reproduce the student sample (filename: *symm.xls*).

10. Model this project for students. Explain to students that they will be following the same steps to create their own designs.

11. Make sure that students know how and where to save their finished work.

12. Give students sufficient time to complete their designs.

13. Allow students to give feedback to one another about this project.

14. Show students how to print their work. First, have students check their work using **Print Preview**. Click **File** on the Menu bar and choose **Print Preview**. If they are satisfied with their work, have them close the **Print Preview** file and print their work.

15. Use the rubric provided on page 22 to assess this lesson.

Extension Ideas

Have students create color cell designs that represent faces. Talk about possible expressions they could create such as happy, sad, surprised, or sleepy.

Have students work in groups to create city or town designs. Have them decide how they will incorporate the idea of symmetry into their buildings, street layouts, and other design components.

Student Directions

1. Open a new workbook.

2. Create a symmetrical design.

3. Choose the right color for your design. Click **Format** on the Menu bar. Click **_Cells..._**

4. Click on the _Patterns_ tab at the top of the Format Cells dialog box.

5. Choose the the right color for your design. Click **OK**.

6. Now, try using the **Fill Color** button on the _Formatting_ toolbar.

7. Click **View** on the Menu bar. Click **_Toolbars>_**. Choose _Formatting_.

8. Select the cells you want to add color to. Click the arrow to right of **Fill Color** button. Choose a color from the palette.

9. Save your work.

10. Print your work. Use the **_Print Preview_** feature first. Click **File** on the Menu bar and choose **_Print Preview_**.

11. Share your work with others.

Assessment Rubric

Strong **(3 Points)**	The student successfully created a symmetrical design using the Fill Color feature.	The student correctly opened, saved, and printed a workbook file.	The student was able to complete his or her work independently.	The student fully understands the lesson objectives.
Effective **(2 Points)**	The student created a symmetrical design using the Fill Color feature.	The student opened, saved, and printed a workbook file.	The student was able to complete his or her work with very little support.	The student mostly understands the lesson objectives.
Emerging **(1 Point)**	The student attempted to create a symmetrical design using the Fill Color feature.	The student attempted to open, save, and print a workbook file.	The student was able to complete his or her work with support.	The student somewhat understands the lesson objectives.
Not Yet **(0 Points)**	The student did not create a symmetrical design using the Fill Color feature.	The student did not open, save, and print a workbook file.	The student was unable to complete his or her work.	The student does not understand the lesson objectives.
Self Score				
Teacher Score				
Total Score				

Comments:

Mystery Fill Designs

Lesson Description

Students follow a list of clues to create colorful designs using *Excel.*

Content Standard

Students understand the concept of geometric constructions.

Technology Skill

Students open and save a new workbook and fill cells with color.

Additional Technology Skills

- using the Menu bar and toolbars
- saving and printing work

Material

- student sample (filename: *myst.xls*)

Teacher Preparation

1. Print and review the student sample (filename: *myst.xls*).

2. Create additional project samples for students to use as extra credit or challenge activities. These can be subject or theme related.

Procedure

1. Explain to the students that they will be learning how to get started using a workbook application. Open *Microsoft Excel.*

2. Open a workbook (or spreadsheet file) and show students that a worksheet has boxes called *cells.* Share examples of the types of things they will learn how to do with this application.

3. Show students how to open and save workbooks. (See page 14.) Emphasize to students that they should save their work often. Discuss how you would like them to name their projects. You may want students to use their names as part of their filenames.

4. Have students open and save their own workbook files.

5. Explain how each cell has a label that has a letter and a number. Highlight different cells and show students how they can tell what a cell's label is. Stress that columns have letter labels and rows have number labels. For example, a cell in Column A and Row 2 is known as A2.

Procedure (*cont.*)

6. Call out a particular cell label and have students find the cell location. Have them check the cell label in the top left corner of their worksheets to make sure their choice is correct. Make sure that the **Formula Bar** is selected so that students can see the cell labels. To do this, click **View** on the Menu bar and choose **Formula Bar**. Continue until the students are able to find particular cells with ease.

7. Show students how to fill a cell with color. (See page 14.) Stress to students that they need to select the cell first before clicking **Format** on the Menu bar or the **Fill Color** button on the *Formatting* toolbar.

8. Have students find particular cells and then add color to those cells.

9. Show students how they can also change the color by clicking on the arrow just to the right of the **Fill Color** button on the *Formatting* toolbar.

10. Explain to students that they are going to use these skills to figure out a riddle. Provide students with the Student Directions on page 25. Explain that there are four clues to the riddle. Ask students to follow the four clues, make a colored design, and then figure out the answer to the riddle.

11. Make sure that students know how and where to save their finished work.

12. Give students sufficient time to complete their designs.

13. Let students give feedback to one another about this project.

14. Show students how to print their work. First, have students check their work using **Print Preview**. Click **File** on the Menu bar and choose **Print Preview**. If they are satisfied with their work, have them close the **Print Preview** file and print their work.

15. Use the rubric provided on page 26 to assess this lesson.

Extension Ideas

Have students create color cell designs that represent a design in nature, such as snowflakes, clouds, trees, or buildings.

Students can create color cell designs that tell stories. This can be assigned as a group project where each group member designs a part of the story, such as characters, a background, or props.

Student Directions

1. Open a new workbook.

2. Use these four clues to create a design. You must successfully create the design and answer the following question: In this design, how many cells are the same color as the first color of the rainbow?

    - Clue 1: The cells in columns A, C, and E and Rows 3, 5, and 7 are filled with the first color of the rainbow.

    - Clue 2: The cells in columns A, C, and E and Rows 4 and 6 are filled with the fifth color of the rainbow.

    - Clue 3: The cells in columns B and D and Rows 4 and 6 are filled with the first color of the rainbow.

    - Clue 4: The cells in columns B and D and Rows 3, 5, and 7 are filled with the fifth color of the rainbow.

3. To choose a color, click **Format** on the Menu bar and click *Cells...*

4. Click on the *Patterns* tab at the top of the Format Cells dialog box.

5. Choose the the right color for your design. Click **OK**.

6. You may also use the **Color Fill** button on the *Formatting* toolbar. Click **View** on the Menu bar, click *Toolbars>*. Choose *Formatting*.

7. Save your work.

8. Print your finished project. Check your work using the *Print Preview* feature first. Click **File** on the Menu bar and choose *Print Preview.*

9. Share your work with others.

Strong **(3 Points)**	The student filled all cells in the exact location required and with the correct color.	The student correctly opened, saved, and printed a workbook file.	The student was able to complete his or her work independently.	The student fully understands the lesson objectives.
Effective **(2 Points)**	The student filled three or four cell groups in the exact location required and with the correct color.	The student opened, saved, and printed a workbook file with little assistance.	The student was able to complete his or her work with little support.	The student mostly understands the lesson objectives.
Emerging **(1 Point)**	The student filled one or two cell groups in the exact location required and with the correct color.	The student opened, saved, and printed a workbook file with assistance.	The student was able to complete his or her work with support.	The student somewhat understands the lesson objectives.
Not Yet **(0 Points)**	Student was unable to locate or fill cells for this project.	The student could not open, save, and print a workbook file.	The student was unable to complete his or her work.	The student does not understand the lesson objectives.
Self Score				
Teacher Score				
Total Score				

Comments:

Text entered within a cell, or multiple cells, can be formatted much as it can be in a word processing program. It is often helpful to change the text font, size, or color to distinguish titles, labels, and values.

Step-by-Step Directions

Changing the Cell Size

1. To change the size of the cells, select them all first. Do this by clicking on the **Select All** button in the top left corner of the worksheet. (On a Macintosh, it looks like a diamond. On a PC, it is an empty square.)

2. To change cell size, click **Format** on the Menu bar, choose **Row** or **Column** and then *Height...* or *Width...* Change the row height or the column width to the desired size and click **OK**.

Changing the Font and Font Size

1. Click in the cell, or select all the cells, where you would like to change the font and/or font size.

2. Click **View** on the Menu bar. Choose **Toolbars >** and then *Formatting*.

3. To change the font, click on the arrow button next to the text box that shows the currently selected font. Click on a font to select it.

4. To change the font size, click the arrow button next to the text box that shows the currently selected font size. Click a font size to select it.

Changing the Font Color and Font Style

1. Click in the cell, or select all the cells, where you would like to change the font color and/or style.

2. To change the font color, go to the *Formatting* toolbar and click the font color button to change the font to the most recently used color as it is displayed in the button.

3. To select a new color, click the arrow just to the right of the font color button. Click on a color.

4. To change the style, click one (or more) of the font style buttons on the *Formatting* toolbar to make the text bold, italic, and/or underlined.

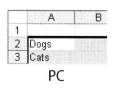
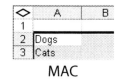

PC   MAC

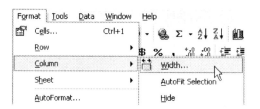

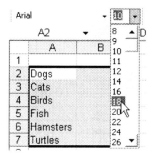

Quick Tip

The font size, style, and color can also be changed by clicking **Format** on the Menu bar. Then, click **Cells...** and a Format Cells dialog box will appear. Click on the *Font* tab. (On a Macintosh: You can choose to use the **Formatting Palette** by clicking **View** on the Menu bar and choosing **Formatting Palette**.)

Spelling Fun

Lesson Description

Students use current spelling words to learn how to format cells and make changes to the text they have entered.

Content Standard

Students use other resources to spell words.

Technology Skill

Students format cells in worksheets.

Additional Technology Skills

- adding text to cells
- adding borders to cells
- saving and printing work

Materials

- list of spelling words
- student sample (filename: *spell.xls*)

Teacher Preparation

1. Print and review the student sample (filename: *spell.xls*).

2. You may want students to work independently, in pairs, or in small groups. Review the procedure and consider various groupings before you begin to teach the lesson.

Procedure

1. Explain to students that they will be using a workbook (or spreadsheet file) application and learning how to format cells. In order to do this, students will use a list of spelling words that they are currently studying.

2. Review opening and saving a workbook, identifying cell labels (A1), and adding color to cells. (See page 14.)

3. Model opening a new workbook.

4. Explain to your students how they can control the look of their worksheets (or spreadsheets). Sometimes they may want to change the look or overall format of their workbooks to something different. Show them that when a workbook opens, the cells are rectangles. Today they will be changing the cells' shapes to squares.

5. Show students how to change all the cells at once. Show them the **Select All** button in the top, left corner of the worksheet. (See page 14.) Explain that when they click this marker and make format changes, those changes will apply to all the cells in the worksheets.

Procedure (*cont.*)

6. Show students how to change the column width and row height. (See page 27.) Change the row height and column width to .40 in./38.4 pixels.

7. Show the students how they can make other changes to the worksheet's format. Show them how to change the font itself, as well as the font size, style, and color. Point out the *Formatting* toolbar and the buttons for each feature. (See page 27.)

8. Explain to the students that for this project they will choose Times for the font style and 20 for the font size. Show them how to make this change to their worksheets.

9. Show students how to add text to cells. In this project, they will be adding their spelling words into the cells. One spelling word will go on each row and one letter will go in each cell. Show students the sample (filename: *spell.xls*) found on the Teacher Resource CD before they begin working independently.

10. Show students how to place borders around each word rather than around each letter. This can be done by selecting one word at a time. To select a word, click on the first letter of the word and drag across to highlight the entire word. Click **Format** on the Menu bar and choose *Cells...* Click the *Border* tab. Under *Presets*, click on the *Outline* icon. Or, students can use the **Borders** button on the *Formatting* toolbar. Choose the first option called **Outside Borders**.

11. Give students sufficient time to use their spelling lists to practice formatting cells. Encourage them to be creative with the font styles and colors they choose. If you prefer, place students in pairs or small groups to practice formatting cells.

12. Show students how to print their work. First, have students check their work using **Print Preview**. Click **File** on the Menu bar and choose **Print Preview**. If they are satisfied with their work, have them close the **Print Preview** file and print their work. Have students share their work with you and with their classmates.

13. Use the rubric provided on page 31 to assess this lesson.

Extension Ideas

Students can code their words by filling the cells with color and/or by adding borders to their words. Suggest that they follow a pattern and not use random colors. For example, a certain color may be used for vowels, beginning letter sounds, or word endings. It is easier to remember words when they follow a predictable visual pattern.

Student Directions

1. Open a new workbook.

2. Click the **Select All** button in the top left corner to highlight the whole worksheet.

3. Click **Format** on the Menu bar. Choose **Column** and then *Width…*

4. Set the column width at .40 in./38.4 pixels. Click **OK**.

5. Click **Format** on the Menu bar. Choose **Row** and then *Height…*

6. Set the row height at .40 in./38.4 pixels. Click **OK**.

7. Find the *Formatting* toolbar. Click **View** on the Menu bar. Click **Toolbars>** and choose *Formatting*.

8. Use the **Font** button on the *Formatting* toolbar to choose the Times font. Use the **Font Size** button to change the size of the font to 20.

9. Type your spelling words. Put one letter in each cell. Start a new row for each word.

10. Check your words to make sure they are all correct. Make any changes you need to make.

11. Highlight each word. Use the **Borders** button on the *Formatting* toolbar to place a border around each word.

12. Use the buttons on the *Formatting* toolbar to change the font color and font style to make the words look interesting.

13. Save and print your work.

14. Share your work with others.

Assessment Rubric

Strong **(3 Points)**	The student used the Select All feature and changed the cell size.	The student correctly changed the font style and size.	The student entered the spelling words correctly and placed borders around the words.	The student fully understands the lesson objectives.
Effective **(2 Points)**	The student used the Select All feature and changed the cell size with some support.	The student changed the font style and size.	The student entered the spelling words correctly and placed borders around most of the words.	The student mostly understands the lesson objectives.
Emerging **(1 Point)**	The student attempted to use the Select All feature and change the cell size.	The student attempted to change the font style and size.	The student attempted to enter the spelling words and placed borders around some of the words.	The student somewhat understands the lesson objectives.
Not Yet **(0 Points)**	The student did not use the Select All feature to change the cell size.	The student did not change the font style and size.	The student did not enter the spelling words correctly and did not place borders around the words.	The student does not understand the lesson objectives.
Self Score				
Teacher Score				
Total Score				
Comments:				

Guess the Word

Lesson Description

Students create and play vocabulary games to learn how to format cells and make changes to the text they have entered.

Content Standard

Students understand reading vocabulary.

Technology Skill

Students format cells in worksheets.

Additional Technology Skills

- adding borders to cells
- adding color to cells
- adding text to cells
- moving between worksheets
- copying and pasting worksheets
- saving work

Materials

- copy of words needed for the project
- student sample (filename: *guess.xls*)

Teacher Preparation

1. Print an example of each of the student samples (filename: *guess.xls*) to show the three steps for student reference. [Note: The three steps are on three different worksheets in the same file. Move between worksheets by clicking on the titles or tabs at the bottom of the screen.]

2. Decide on student pairs for this activity.

3. Create word lists for this project. Students may all use the same words, or you may have them use different words.

Procedure

1. Explain to the students that they will be using a workbook application to learn how to format cells. In order to do this, students will create and play vocabulary games.

2. Review opening and saving a workbook, identifying cell labels (A1), and adding color to cells. (See page 14.) Model opening a new file.

3. Show your students how they can control the look of their worksheets (or spreadsheets). Sometimes they may want to change the look or format of their worksheets to something different. Show them that when a worksheet opens, the cells are rectangles. Today, they will be changing the cells' shapes to squares.

4. Show students that they can change all the cells at once with the **Select All** button in the top, left corner of the worksheet. Explain that when they click this and then make format changes, those changes will apply to all the cells in their worksheets.

Procedure (*cont.*)

5. Show students how to change the row height and column width to .40 in./38.4 pixels. (See page 27.)

6. Show the students how they can make other changes to the worksheet's format. Show them how to change the font itself, as well as the font size, style, and color. Point out the *Formatting* toolbar and the buttons for each feature. (See page 27.)

7. Explain to the students that for this project they will use Times font for the font style and 20 for the font size. Show them how to make this change.

8. Show students how to add text to cells. In this project, students will create vocabulary games that they will play with a partner. They will type five words into the cells; one word per row with one letter in each cell.

9. Show students the Project Step 1 worksheet from the student sample (filename: *guess.xls*). [Note: You will see the label on the tabs at the bottom of the screen.] Have them type their five words. Point out that they will leave two blank rows between each word.

10. Show students the Project Step 2 worksheet. Explain that they will enter an answer below each vocabulary word. These answers need to be *antonyms*. Review what an antonym is. Students will then use the *Formatting* toolbar to fill the answer cells with red. (See page 14.) They will then place borders around each cell in the answers. (See page 29, step 10.) These will be the answer sheets.

11. Show students the Project Step 3 worksheet. Show them how to copy and paste their answer sheets onto new worksheets. Click **Edit** on the Menu bar. Choose **Move or Copy Sheet...** Make sure that the *Create a copy* box is checked at the bottom of the Move or Copy dialog box. Then, select *(move to the end)*. Click **OK**.

12. This will be the game version of their projects. Have them change the answer text color to red to match the cell fill.

13. Show students how to play the game. Working in pairs, each student will take turns calling out letters. They will highlight a cell and change the color back to black when a correct letter is called. They can create records of the letters used on the bottom of the sheets.

14. Give students sufficient time to type their word lists, answer sheets, and game versions.

15. Have students work in pairs and play their games.

16. Use the rubric provided on page 35 to assess this lesson.

Extension Idea

Have students create new games with different words. They may be related to different topics of study or books.

Student Directions

1. Open a new workbook.

2. Click the **Select All** button to highlight the entire worksheet.

3. Click **Format** on the Menu bar. Choose **Column** and then *Width...* Set the column width at .40 in./38.4 pixels.

4. Click **Format** on the Menu bar. Choose *Row* and then *Height...* Set the row height at .40 in./38.4 pixels.

5. Find the *Formatting* toolbar. Click **View** on the Menu bar. Click *Toolbars>* and choose *Formatting*.

6. Use the *Formatting* toolbar to choose the Times font and to set the font size at 20.

7. Enter your words. Place one letter in each cell. Start a new row for each word. Leave two blank rows between each word.

8. Enter your answers below your game words. Use the **Color Fill** button on the *Formatting* toolbar to color the answer cells red.

9. Use the **Borders** button on the *Formatting* toolbar to place borders around each letter in each answer. This will be your answer sheet.

10. Copy your answer sheet. Paste it onto a new worksheet. Click **Edit** on the Menu bar. Choose **Move or Copy Sheet...** Make sure that the *Create a copy* box is checked. Select *(move to the end)* and click **OK**.

11. Use the **Font Color** button on the *Formatting* toolbar to change the text color for each answer to the same color as its background cell color. This will be your game sheet.

12. Save your work.

13. Play your game with your partner. As correct letters are guessed, change the font color back to black. You may add any incorrect letters that your partner guesses to the bottom of the game sheet. This way, your partner will know what letters have been used as the game progresses.

Assessment Rubric

Strong **(3 Points)**	The student used the Select All feature and changed the cell size correctly.	The student correctly changed the font style and size.	The student entered the spelling words correctly and placed the borders.	The student correctly created a game sheet and an answer sheet.	The student fully understands the lesson objectives.
Effective **(2 Points)**	The student used the Select All feature and changed the cell size correctly with some support.	The student changed the font style and size.	The student entered the spelling words and placed the borders.	The student created a game sheet and an answer sheet.	The student mostly understands the lesson objectives.
Emerging **(1 Point)**	The student attempted to use the Select All feature and change the cell size.	The student attempted to change the font style and size.	The student attempted to enter the spelling words and place the borders.	The student attempted to create a game sheet and an answer sheet.	The student somewhat understands the lesson objectives.
Not Yet **(0 Points)**	The student did not use the Select All feature to change the cell size.	The student did not change the font style and size.	The student did not enter the spelling words and/or did not place the borders.	The student did not create a game sheet and an answer sheet.	The student does not understand the lesson objectives.
Self Score					
Teacher Score					
Total Score					
Comments:					

Crossword Puzzle

Lesson Description

Students create crossword puzzles to learn how to format cells and make changes to the text they have entered.

Content Standard

Students use graphic representations to organize information and ideas.

Technology Skill

Students format cells in worksheets.

Additional Technology Skills

- adding borders to cells
- adding color to cells
- adding text to cells
- moving between worksheets
- copying and pasting worksheets
- saving and printing work

Materials

- student copies of words for the project
- student sample (filename: *cross.xls*)

Teacher Preparation

1. Print and review the student sample (filename: *cross.xls*).

2. Create additional project samples for students to use as extra credit or challenge activities. These can be subject or theme related.

Procedure

1. Explain to your students that they will be using a workbook application to create crossword puzzles.

2. Review opening and saving a workbook (or spreadsheet file), identifying cell labels (A1), and adding color to cells. (See page 14.)

3. Model opening a new file.

4. Show your students how they can control the look of their worksheets (or spreadsheets). Sometimes they may want to change the look or overall format of their worksheets to something different. Show them that when a worksheet opens, the cells are rectangles. Today, they will be changing the cells' shapes to squares.

5. Show students that they can change all the cells. Show them the **Select All** button on the top, left corner of the worksheet. Explain that when they select this marker and make format changes, those changes will apply to all the cells in their worksheets.

Procedure (*cont.*)

6. Show students how to change the row height and column width. (See page 27.) Change the row height and column width to .40 in./38.4 pixels.

7. Show students how they can make other changes to the worksheet's format. Show them how to change the font itself, as well as the font size, style, and color. Point out the *Formatting* toolbar and the buttons for each feature. (See page 27.)

8. Explain to the students that for this project they will choose the Times font and a font size of 20.

9. Show students how to add text to cells. In this project, they will be creating their word lists with clues first and then they will make crossword puzzles out of the words. In the puzzles, they will be putting one letter in each cell and the letters of the words will either go down or across the worksheet. They will also overlap.

10. Show students the student sample (filename: *cross.xls*). Working independently, students will create their lists first (with words and definition clues) and then place their words into the puzzle format. Have them use six words (three will go down and three will go across).

11. Show students how to make the number markers for down and across using white numbers and filling the cells with black using the *Formatting* toolbar. (See page 14.)

12. Have the students place borders around the letters in the puzzles. (See page 29, step10.)

13. Show the finished sample puzzle to the students. Demonstrate how to make the second part.

14. Tell students that they will copy their puzzles and paste them on new worksheets. These will be the puzzles others will solve. Then, have students delete the puzzle words from the definition clues. Next, have them delete the answers, leaving the cells white. Make sure students understand that they need to leave the borders on the cells where letters were. Give students sufficient time to create their puzzles.

15. Students can solve this puzzle on the computer, or the puzzles can be printed and solved by hand.

16. Show students how to print their work. First, have students check their work using **Print Preview**. Click **File** on the Menu bar and choose **Print Preview**. If they are satisfied with their work, have them close the **Print Preview** feature and print their work.

17. Use the rubric provided on page 39 to assess students' work.

Extension Idea

Have students create their own crossword puzzles. Have them select themes related to books they have read, or social studies or science topics.

Student Directions

1. Open a new workbook.

2. Click the **Select All** button to highlight the entire worksheet.

3. Click **Format** on the Menu bar. Choose **Column** and then *Width...* Set the column width at .40 in./38.4 pixels.

4. Click **Format** on the Menu bar. Choose **Row** and then *Height...* Set the row height at .40 in./38.4 pixels.

5. Find the *Formatting* toolbar. Click **View** on the Menu bar. Click **Toolbars>** and choose *Formatting*.

6. Use the *Formatting* toolbar to choose the Times font and to set the font size at 20.

7. Type your crossword puzzle words and clues.

8. Place your word letters on your puzzle. You will have three words down and three words across.

9. Place a border around each letter using the **Borders** button on the *Formatting* toolbar.

10. Add number references. Use the *Formatting* toolbar to use a black cell fill and a white font color. This will be your answer sheet.

11. Click **Edit** on the Menu bar. Choose **Move or Copy Sheet...** Make sure that the **Create a copy** box is checked. Select (*move to the end*) and click **OK**.

12. Delete the words and leave the definitions as clues.

13. Delete the letters for each word on the puzzle. Leave the cell border around each letter space. This will be your puzzle game sheet.

14. Save your work.

15. Play your game with your classmates.

16. Print your work.

Assessment Rubric

Strong **(3 Points)**	The student used the Select All feature and changed the cell size.	The student correctly changed the font style and size.	The student entered the words correctly and placed a border around each letter.	The student correctly created a game sheet and an answer sheet.	The student fully understands the lesson objectives.
Effective **(2 Points)**	The student used the Select All feature and changed the cell size with some support.	The student changed the font style and size.	The student entered the words and placed a border around most of the letters.	The student created a game sheet and an answer sheet.	The student mostly understands the lesson objectives.
Emerging **(1 Point)**	The student attempted to use the Select All feature and change the cell size.	The student attempted to change the font style and size.	The student entered the words and placed a border around some of the letters.	The student attempted to create a game sheet and an answer sheet.	The student somewhat understands the lesson objectives.
Not Yet **(0 Points)**	The student did not use the Select All feature and did not change the cell size.	The student did not change the font style and size.	The student did not enter the spelling words and did not place a border around the letters.	The student did not create a game sheet and an answer sheet.	The student does not understand the lesson objectives.
Self Score					
Teacher Score					
Total Score					
Comments:					

Microsoft Excel offers several formatting options to help you make the text and the data within cells appear the way you want it to. Wrapping text, for example, will keep the cell contents within the width of the cell. Merging cells is an easy way to combine cells when necessary.

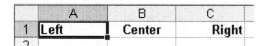

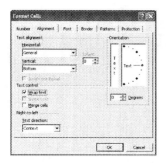

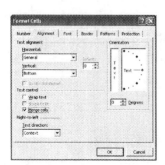

Step-by-Step Directions

Aligning the Contents of a Cell

1. Select the cell or cells you want to align.

2. On the *Formatting* toolbar, click one of the three align buttons (**Align Left** aligns contents to the left of the cell, **Align Center** centers the contents of the cell, and **Align Right** aligns contents to the right of the cell). The *Formatting* toolbar can be found by clicking on **View**, choosing **Toolbars >** and then *Formatting*.

Wrapping Text Within a Cell

1. Click the cell, or cells, in which you want the text to wrap.

2. Click **Format** on the Menu bar.

3. Choose *Cells...*

4. On the Format Cells dialog box, click on the *Alignment* tab to bring it to the forefront.

5. Under *Text Control*, click the *Wrap text* box.

6. Click **OK**.

Merging Cells

1. Select the cells you want to merge, or combine into one.

2. Click **Format** on the Menu bar

3. Choose *Cells...*

4. On the Format Cells dialog box, click on the *Alignment* tab to bring it to the forefront.

5. Under *Text Control*, click the *Merge Cells* box.

6. Click **OK**.

Quick Tip

You can also merge cells by using the **Merge and Center** button on the *Formatting* toolbar.

Favorite Animal

Lesson Description

Students change the rows and columns in a worksheet as they record and organize information about their favorite animals.

Content Standard

Students know that differences exist among individuals of the same kind of animal.

Technology Skill

Students will change rows and columns in a worksheet.

Additional Technology Skills

- adding color to cells
- adding text to cells
- changing the font and the font size
- saving and printing work

Materials

- books and other resources about animals
- student sample (filename: *anim.xls*)

Teacher Preparation

1. Print and review the student sample (filename: *anim.xls*).

2. You may want students to work independently, in pairs, or in small groups. Review the procedure and consider various groupings before you begin to teach the lesson.

Procedure

1. Explain to students that they will be using a workbook (or spreadsheet) application to organize information about their favorite animals.

2. Open a new workbook. Review how to use the **Select All** button to change the font to Times and the font size to 14. (See page 27.)

3. Demonstrate to students how to create titles for their projects. Type a title into the first cell in the first row (A1). Once you have entered a title, discuss how to merge cells. Show them how to select the first two cells in row 1 (A1 and B1). Then, select the **Merge and Center** button on the *Formatting* toolbar to merge the A1 and B1 cells into one cell. (See page 40.) Remember, to find the *Formatting* toolbar, click **View** on the Menu bar, choose **Toolbars >** and then *Formatting*.

4. Next, show students how to enter titles. They will be putting these two titles into two columns: *Animals* and *Fun Facts*. To begin, suggest a column cell width of 2 in./192 pixels.

Procedure (cont.)

5. Show students how to enter each column title into its own cell. Then, show them how to bold and center the titles within each cell. Point out the **Align Center** button on the *Formatting* toolbar. (See page 40.) Also, remind students where the **Bold** button is located on the *Formatting* toolbar. (See page 27.)

6. Show students how to set the column width and the row height at 2 in./192 pixels.

. (See page 27.)

7. Once titles are in place, students can enter their animals and fun facts. Explain horizontal and vertical alignment, text wrap, and text direction. Have students click **Format** on the Menu bar and choose **Cells...** In the Format Cells dialog box, have students click on the *Alignment* tab. Show students how to center, align, and wrap text in the cells. (See page 40.)

8. Model using the **Fill Color** button on the *Formatting* toolbar to shade the rows and columns with color. (See page 14.)

9. Show students the student sample (filename: *anim.xls*) found on the Teacher Resource CD before they begin working independently. Give students sufficient time to finish their projects. You can decide on the number of animals you would like students to include in their work.

10. Encourage them to be creative with the cell fill colors they choose.

11. When students are finished, have them save their work.

12. Show students how to print their work. First, have students check their work using **Print Preview**. Click **File** on the Menu bar and choose **Print Preview**. If they are satisfied with their work, have them close the **Print Preview** feature and print their work.

13. Have students share their work with you and their classmates.

14. Use the rubric provided on page 44 to assess this lesson.

Extension Idea

Students can use this format for other assignments including book reports and other types of research projects.

Student Directions

1. Open a new workbook.

2. Click the **Select All** button to highlight the whole worksheet.

3. Find the *Formatting* toolbar. Click **View** on the Menu bar. Click **Toolbars>** and choose *Formatting*. Use this toolbar to choose the Times font and to set the font size at 14.

4. Type your title into the first cell in the first row (A1). Make the font size of the title is 20.

5. Merge your cells into one title cell. Highlight the two cells (A1 and B1). Click the **Merge and Center** button on the *Formatting* toolbar.

6. Below your title, type your column titles. They are *Animals* and *Fun Facts*.

7. Highlight all text and click the **Align Center** and **Bold** buttons on the *Formatting* toolbar.

8. Set the column width. Highlight the two columns. Click **Format** on the Menu bar. Choose **Column** and then *Width...* Set the column width at 2 in./192 pixels.

9. Set the row height. Click **Format** on the Menu bar. Choose **Row** and then *Height...* Set the row height at 2 in./192 pixels.

10. Type in your text information.

11. Use the **Color Fill** button on the *Formatting* toolbar to add color.

12. Center and wrap your text. Click **Format** on the Menu bar and choose **Cells...** Select the *Alignment* tab. Choose *Center* under *Vertical* alignment and *Center* under *Horizontal* alignment. Check the *Wrap Text* box.

13. Save and print your work.

Assessment Rubric

Strong **(3 Points)**	The student made all the formatting changes necessary to change rows and columns.	The student included accurate information.	The student entered all of the text correctly.	The student fully understands the lesson objectives.
Effective **(2 Points)**	The student made most of the formatting changes necessary to change rows and columns.	The student included mostly accurate information.	The student entered most of the text correctly.	The student understands the lesson objectives.
Emerging **(1 Point)**	The student made some of the formatting changes necessary to change rows and columns.	The student included some accurate information.	The student entered some of the text correctly.	The student somewhat understands the lesson objectives.
Not Yet **(0 Points)**	The student did not make the formatting changes necessary to change rows and columns.	The student included inaccurate information.	The student did not enter the text correctly.	The student does not understand the lesson objectives.
Self Score				
Teacher Score				
Total Score				

Comments:

Cloud Information Chart

Lesson Description

Students change the rows and columns in worksheets as they record and organize information about clouds and related weather.

Content Standard

Students know that water exists in the air in different forms.

Technology Skill

Students will change rows and columns in worksheets.

Additional Technology Skills

- adding color to cells
- adding text to cells
- changing the font and the font size
- inserting images
- saving and printing work

Materials

- related images downloaded and saved in a folder
- books and other resources about weather, clouds, or other topics of study
- student sample (filename: *cloud.xls*)

Teacher Preparation

1. Print and review the student sample (filename: *cloud.xls*).

2. Review and copy images for student use. Create a folder that is accessible to students.

3. Gather books and other resources for this lesson.

Procedure

1. Explain to the students that they will be using a workbook application to organize information about clouds.

2. Open a new workbook (or spreadsheet file). Review how to use the **Select All** button to change the font to Times and the font size to 12. (See page 27.)

3. Demonstrate to students how to create titles for their projects. Type a title into the first cell in the first row (A1) using font size 20. Once you have entered a title, discuss how to merge cells. Show them how to select the first four cells in row 1 (A1, B1, C1 and D1). Then, click on the **Merge and Center** button on the *Formatting* toolbar to merge the four cells into one cell. (See page 40.) Remember, to find the *Formatting* toolbar, click on **View**, choose **Toolbars >** and then *Formatting*.

4. Next, show students how to enter titles. They will be putting these four titles into four columns: *Cloud Type, Photo, Cloud Level* and *Related Weather*.

Procedure *(cont.)*

5. Show students how to enter each column title into its own cell. Then, show students how to bold and center those titles. Point out the **Bold** and **Align Center** buttons on the *Formatting* toolbar. (See pages 27 and 40 respectively.)

6. Show students how to set the column width and row height to 2 in./192 pixels. (See page 27.)

7. Once titles are in place, students can enter their facts about clouds. Explain horizontal and vertical alignment, text wrap, and text direction. Remind students to click **Format** on the Menu bar, choose **Cells...** and then select the *Alignment* tab. Show students how to center, align, and wrap text in the cells.

8. Model using the **Fill Color** button on the *Formatting* toolbar to shade the rows and columns with color. (See page 14.)

9. Next, show students how to insert photos. They will click **Insert** on the Menu bar, choose **Picture**, and then choose *From File...* to place images in the appropriate cells on the worksheets. Be sure to follow your school's policy for citing images.

10. Show students how to adjust the size of their images manually by dragging the corner arrow of the selected images.

11. Give students sufficient time to finish their projects. Show students the student sample (filename: *cloud.xls*) before they begin working independently. You can decide on the number of examples you would like students to include in their work.

12. Encourage students to be creative with the cell fill colors they choose.

13. When students are finished, have them save their work.

14. Show students how to print their work. First, have students check their work using **Print Preview**. Click **File** on the Menu bar and choose **Print Preview**. If they are satisfied with their work, have them close the **Print Preview** feature and print their work.

15. Have students share their work with you and with their classmates.

16. Use the rubric provided on page 48 to assess this lesson.

Extension Ideas

Students can use this format for science and social studies reports as well as book reports.

Student Directions

1. Open a new workbook.

2. Click the **Select All** button to highlight the entire worksheet.

3. Find the *Formatting* toolbar. Click **View** on the Menu bar. Click **Toolbars>** and choose *Formatting*. Use this toolbar to choose the Times font and to set the font size at 12.

4. Type your title in the first cell in the first row (A1). Make the font size of the title 20.

5. Select the first four cells (A1, B1, C1 and D1). Using the **Merge and Center** button on the *Formatting* toolbar, merge these cells into one.

6. Type your column titles. They are *Cloud Type*, *Photo*, *Cloud Level*, and *Related Weather*.

7. Select all the titles and click the **Align Center** and **Bold** buttons on the *Formatting* toolbar.

8. Set the column width at 2 in./192 pixels. Highlight the four columns. Click **Format** on the Menu bar. Choose **Column** and then *Width…*

9. Set the row height at 2 in./192 pixels. Highlight the number of rows you will use. Click **Format** on the Menu bar. Choose **Row** and then *Height…*

10. Type in your text information.

11. Use the **Color Fill** button on the *Formatting* toolbar to add color to rows and columns.

12. Center and wrap your text. Click **Format** on the Menu bar, choose **Cells…** Click the *Alignment* tab. Choose *Center* under *Vertical* and *Center* under *Horizontal*. Check the *Wrap Text* box.

13. Add your images. Click **Insert** on the Menu bar. Choose **Picture >** and then *From File…* Adjust the size of your image by dragging the corner arrow of the selected image.

14. Save and print your work.

Assessment Rubric

Strong **(3 Points)**	The student made all the formatting changes necessary to change rows and columns.	The student included accurate information and images.	The student entered all text correctly.	The student fully understands the lesson objectives.
Effective **(2 Points)**	The student made most of the formatting changes necessary to change rows and columns.	The student included mostly accurate information and images.	The student entered most of the text correctly.	The student understands the lesson objectives.
Emerging **(1 Point)**	The student made some of the formatting changes necessary to change rows and columns.	The student included some accurate information and images.	The student entered some of the text correctly.	The student somewhat understands the lesson objectives.
Not Yet **(0 Points)**	The student did not make any of the formatting changes necessary to change rows and columns.	The student included inaccurate information and images.	The student did not enter the text correctly.	The student does not understand the lesson objectives.
Self Score				
Teacher Score				
Total Score				

Comments:

Planet Comparison Chart

Lesson Description

Students change the rows and columns in worksheets as they record and organize information about planets.

Content Standard

Students know the characteristics of the eight planets in our solar system.

Technology Skill

Students will change rows and columns in worksheets.

Additional Technology Skills

- adding color to cells
- adding text to cells
- changing the font and the font size
- inserting images
- saving and printing work

Materials

- related photos for the project
- books and other resources about planets
- student sample (filename: *planet.xls*)

Teacher Preparation

1. Print and review the student sample (filename: *planet.xls*).

2. Review and copy images for student use. Create a folder that is accessible for students.

3. Gather books and any other necessary resources for this lesson.

Procedure

1. Explain to the students that they will be using a workbook (or spreadsheet) application to organize information about planets.

2. Open a new workbook. Review how to use the **Select All** button to change the font to Times and the font size to 14. (See page 27.)

3. Demonstrate how to create a title for a project. Type a title into the first column in the first row (A1) using a font size of 20. Once you have entered a title, discuss how to merge cells. Show them how to select the first three cells in row 1 (A1, B1, and C1). Then, have students click on the **Merge and Center** button on the *Formatting* toolbar to merge the three cells into one cell. (See page 40.) Remember, to find the *Formatting* toolbar, click on **View**, choose *Toolbars >* and then *Formatting*.

4. Next, show students how to enter titles. They will be putting these four titles into columns: *Planet Name, Photo, Diameter in Miles,* and *Distance from the Sun in Miles.*

Procedure *(cont.)*

5. Set the row height at .5 in./48 pixels for the top two title rows. Set the row height for the planet rows at 2 in./192 pixels. (See page 27.)

6. Show students how to enter each column title into its cell and bold and center the titles of those cells. Point out the **Bold** and **Align Center** buttons on the *Formatting* toolbar. (See pages 27 and 40 respectively.)

7. Once titles are in place, students can enter their facts about the planets. Explain horizontal and vertical alignment, text wrap, and text direction. Show students how to click **Format** on the Menu bar and choose **Cells...** Then, select the *Alignment* tab. Show students how to center text, align text, and wrap text in the cells.

8. Show students how to use the **Fill Color** button on the *Formatting* toolbar to shade the rows and columns with color. (See page 14.)

9. Show students how to insert images. To place an image into the appropriate cell on the worksheet, click **Insert** on the Menu bar, choose **Picture** and then *From File...* Be sure to follow your school's policy for citing images.

10. Show students how to manually adjust the size of an image by dragging the corner arrow of the selected image.

11. Give students sufficient time to finish their projects.

12. Show students the student sample (filename: *planet.xls*) before they begin working independently. Decide on the number of examples you would like students to include in their work.

13. Encourage them to be creative with the cell fill colors they choose.

14. When students are finished, have them save their work.

15. Show students how to print their work. First, have students check their work using **Print Preview**. Click **File** on the Menu bar and choose **Print Preview**. If they are satisfied with their work, have them close the **Print Preview** feature and print their work.

16. Have students share their work with you and with their classmates.

17. Use the rubric provided on page 52 to assess this lesson.

Extension Ideas

Students can use this format to organize information about other items in the solar system, including the sun, meteors, and comets.

Student Directions

1. Open a new workbook.

2. Click the **Select All** button to highlight the entire worksheet.

3. Find the *Formatting* toolbar. Click **View** on the Menu bar. Click **Toolbars>** and choose *Formatting*. Use this toolbar to choose the Times font and to set the font size at 12.

4. Type your title into the first cell in the first row (A1). Make the font size of the title 20.

5. Select the first four cells (A1, B1, C1, and D1). Click the **Merge and Center** button on the *Formatting* toolbar. Merge your four cells into one title cell.

6. Type in your column titles. They are *Planet Name*, *Photo*, *Diameter in Miles*, and *Distance from the Sun in Miles*.

7. Click the **Align Center** and **Bold** buttons on the *Formatting* toolbar.

8. Set the column width. First, highlight the four columns. Click **Format** on the Menu bar. Choose **Column** and then **Width...** Set the column width at 2 in./192 pixels.

9. Set the row height. The first two rows can be .5 in./48 pixels. The other rows can be 2 in./192 pixels. Click **Format** on the Menu bar. Choose **Row** and then *Height...*

10. Type in your text information.

11. Use the **Color Fill** button on the *Formatting* toolbar to add color to your rows and columns.

12. Click **Format** on the Menu bar and choose **Cells...** Then, select the *Alignment* tab. Choose *Center* under *Vertical* and *Center* under *Horizontal*. Check the *Wrap Text* box.

13. Add your images. Click **Insert** on the Menu bar and choose **Picture** and then *From File...*

14. Adjust the size of your image. You can do this by dragging the corner arrow of the selected image.

15. Save your work. Print your work. Share your work.

Strong **(3 Points)**	The student made all the formatting changes necessary to change rows and columns.	The student included accurate information and images.	The student entered all of the text correctly.	The student fully understands the lesson objectives.
Effective **(2 Points)**	The student made most of the formatting changes necessary to change rows and columns.	The student included mostly accurate information and images.	The student entered most of the text correctly.	The student understands the lesson objectives.
Emerging **(1 Point)**	The student made some of the formatting changes necessary to change rows and columns.	The student included some accurate information and images.	The student entered some of the text correctly.	The student somewhat understands the lesson objectives.
Not Yet **(0 Points)**	The student did not make the formatting changes necessary to change rows and columns.	The student included inaccurate information and images.	The student did not enter any of the text correctly.	The student does not understand the lesson objectives.
Self Score				
Teacher Score				
Total Score				
Comments:				

One of the most powerful features of *Microsoft Excel* is its ability to help quickly sort and organize data. Using the sort tool, you can sort text by putting names in alphabetical order, or you can sort numeric data in either ascending or descending order according to size.

Step-by-Step Directions

Sorting Lists

1. Select the cells containing the data you want to sort.

2. Click **Data** on the Menu bar.

3. Choose *Sort...*

4. On the Sort dialog box, click the *Sort by* list arrow. Then, select the first column you want to sort.

5. Click *Ascending* or *Descending* depending on the order you want the data. For numeric data, descending order means from the highest number to the lowest number and ascending means from the lowest number to the highest number. For text, ascending means from A to Z, while descending means from Z to A.

6. If you are only sorting data based on one column, click **OK**. If not, continue to the next step.

7. Click the *Then by* list arrow and select the second column you want to sort.

8. Click *Ascending* or *Descending* depending on the order you want the data.

9. Click **OK** if you are finished, or repeat steps 7 and 8 to specify the third column and the order in which you want to sort your data.

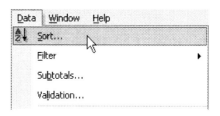

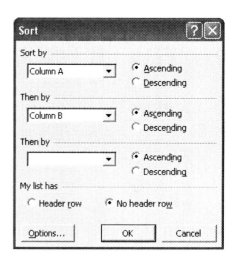

Quick Tip

To sort by days of the week or months of the year, click **Options...** in the Sort dialog box and select the order you want using the arrow to the right of the *First key sort order* box.

Reading List

Lesson Description

Students create reading lists and sort them alphabetically.

Content Standard

Students read fiction appropriate to grades K–2.

Technology Skill

Students know how to sort lists in a workbook application.

Additional Technology Skills

- adding color to cells
- adding text
- changing the font and the font size
- saving and printing work

Materials

- copy of book lists
- student sample (filename: *list.xls*)

Teacher Preparation

1. Print and review the student sample (filename: *list.xls*). [Note: There are different worksheets that show different sorts.]

2. You may want students to work independently, in pairs, or in small groups. Review the procedure and consider various groupings before you begin to teach the lesson.

Procedure

1. Explain to students that they will be using a workbook application to create lists of the books they have read. They will list the books and rate them on a scale of 1–10 according to how much they liked each book.

2. Open a new workbook (or spreadsheet file).

3. Explain to students that they will always need to think about the layout of worksheets (or spreadsheets) before they begin to create them. It is important for them to know what their worksheets are going to display, what the format will be, and what they will need to change to accommodate for the parameters of the assignment. Describe the information they will use for these worksheets. Students will be creating a text-based column for the book list and a number-based column to record the books' ratings.

4. Review how to use the **Select All** button to change the font to Times and the font size to 14. Show students how to set the row height to .5 in./48 pixels. (See page 27.) These two settings will be the same for the entire worksheet.

Procedure (cont.)

5. Explain to your students that the other settings will not apply to the entire worksheet so they will not use the **Select All** button. Show students how to set their first column width, for the book name, to 3 in./288 pixels and to set the second column, for the rating, to 2 in./192 pixels. (See page 27.)

6. Model entering the two column headings, *Book Name* and *Rating/10* at the top of each column. Then, show your students how to enter the text information for their book titles and numbers for their ratings.

7. Have students use the **Fill Color** button on the *Formatting* toolbar to shade rows and columns with color. (See page 14.) You may want students to align the text in a certain way. Use the buttons on the *Formatting* toolbar to do so. (See pages 27 and 40.)

8. Show students how to sort data. They will learn to do an *alphabetical sort*. First, focus on selecting the columns and rows involved. Since the title is not part of the sort, point out to students that they should not select it. When the correct columns and rows are selected, click **Data** on the Menu bar and choose **Sort...** Show students how to select the direction of the sort to make it an *ascending sort*. This will place the data in alphabetical order. Have students check to make sure they have the correct column selected in the *Sort By* box. They should sort by *Book Name* first. If you would like, they can then sort by *Rating/10* next using *numerical sort*.

9. Show students the student sample (filename: *list.xls*).

10. Give students sufficient time to finish their projects. You can decide on the number of books you would like students to include in their work.

11. Encourage them to be creative with the cell fill colors they choose.

12. Show students how to print their work. First, have students check their work using **Print Preview**. Click **File** on the Menu bar and choose **Print Preview**. If they are satisfied with their work, have them close the **Print Preview** feature and print their work.

13. Have students share their work with you and their classmates.

14. Use the rubric provided on page 57 to assess this lesson.

Extension Ideas

This lesson can easily be extended with different topics. Vocabulary and spelling lists can be sorted. A time line can be created using dates and event descriptions. Students can also record authors and book titles and sort that information in a variety of ways.

Student Directions

1. Open a new workbook.

2. Click the **Select All** button to highlight the whole worksheet.

3. Find Find the *Formatting* toolbar. Click **View** on the Menu bar. Click **Toolbars>** and choose *Formatting*. Use this toolbar to choose the Times font and to set the font size at 14.

4. Change the row height. Click **Format** on the Menu bar. Choose **Row**. Choose *Height…* Set the height at .5 in./48 pixels.

5. Select the first column, *Book Name*. Click **Format** on the Menu bar. Choose **Column** and then *Width…* Set the width at 3 in./288 pixels.

6. Do the same for the second column, *Rating/10*. Set the width at 2 in./192 pixels.

7. Type your column headings: *Book Name* and *Rating/10*.

8. Type each book title and its rating. Check your work carefully.

9. Add color to your rows and columns. Use the **Color Fill** button on the *Formatting* toolbar.

10. Select the rows and titles with your data. Click **Data** on the Menu bar. Choose **Sort…** Sort your data alphabetically by choosing *Ascending*.

11. Save your list.

12. Print your work. Check **Print Preview** first. It is under **File** on the Menu bar. Share your work with others.

Assessment Rubric

Strong (3 Points)	The student created and formatted the worksheet correctly.	The student entered all of the text correctly.	The student printed the worksheet correctly.	The student fully understands the lesson objectives.
Effective (2 Points)	The student created and formatted most of the worksheet correctly.	The student entered most of the text correctly.	The student printed the worksheet.	The student understands the lesson objectives.
Emerging (1 Point)	The student created and formatted some of the worksheet correctly.	The student entered some of the text correctly.	The student attempted to print the worksheet.	The student somewhat understands the lesson objectives.
Not Yet (0 Points)	The student did not create and format the worksheet correctly.	The student did not enter text correctly.	The student was unable to print the worksheet.	The student does not understand the lesson objectives.
Self Score				
Teacher Score				
Total Score				

Comments:

Book List

Lesson Description

Students create book lists and sort them alphabetically and numerically.

Content Standard

Students read fiction appropriate to grades 3–5.

Technology Skill

Students know how to sort lists in a workbook application.

Additional Technology Skills

- adding color to cells
- adding textt
- changing the font and the font size
- saving and printing work

Materials

- copy of book lists
- student sample (filename: *book.xls*)

Teacher Preparation

1. Print and review the student sample (filename: *book.xls*). [Note: There are different worksheets that show different sorts.]

2. You may want students to work independently, in pairs, or in small groups. Review the procedure and consider various groupings before you begin to teach the lesson.

Procedure

1. Explain to the students that they will be using a workbook (or spreadsheet) application to create lists of the books they have read. They will list the book titles, their authors, the dates read, and book ratings on a scale of 1–10.

2. Open a new workbook (spreadsheet file).

3. Explain to students that they will always need to think about the layout of worksheets before they begin to create them. It is important for them to know what their worksheets are going to display, what the format will be, and what they will need to change to accommodate the parameters of the assignment. Describe the information they will use for their worksheets. Students will be creating text-based columns for the book titles and author lists, date-based columns for the dates, and number-based columns to record the books' ratings.

4. Review how to use the **Select All** button to change the font to Times and the font size to 14. Show students how to set the row height to .5 in./48 pixels. (See page 27.) These two settings will be the same for the entire worksheet.

Procedure (*cont.*)

5. Explain to your students that the other settings will not apply to the entire worksheet so they will not use the **Select All** button. Show students how to set their first column widths, for the book names, to 3 in./288 pixels. Model setting the second and third columns, for the authors and dates, to 2 in./192 pixels. Finally, set the fourth column, for the ratings, to 1.5 in./144 pixels (See page 27.)

6. Model entering the column headings: *Book Name*, *Author*, *Date Read*, and *Rating/10*. Then, enter sample data. Show students how to enter the text information for their book titles and authors, date information for the dates read, and numbers for the book ratings.

7. Show students how to use the **Fill Color** button on the *Formatting* toolbar to shade the rows and columns with color. (See page 14.)

8. If you want students to align text in a certain way, use the buttons on the *Formatting* toolbar. (See page 40.)

9. Show students how to sort data. They will learn how to do an alphabetical sort. First, focus on selecting the columns and rows involved. Since the title is not part of the sort, be sure to point out that students should not select it. Next, click **Data** on the Menu bar and choose **Sort...** Show students how to select the direction of the sort to make it an *ascending sort* or a *descending sort*. Have students check to make sure they have the correct columns selected in the **Sort By** box.

10. Share with students the student sample (filename: *book.xls*).

11. Model sorting the data, first alphabetically by book and/or author and then numerically by the rating. Have them use the *numerical sort* for printing.

12. Give students sufficient time to finish their projects. You can decide on the number of books you would like students to include in their work. Encourage them to be creative with the cell fill colors they choose.

13. When students are finished, have them save and print their work. Have students check **Print Preview** under **File** on the Menu bar before printing their worksheets.

14. Have students share their work with you and their classmates.

15. Use the rubric provided on page 61 to assess this lesson.

Extension Ideas

This lesson can easily be extended with different topics. Vocabulary and spelling lists can be sorted. A time line can be created using dates and event descriptions. Students can also record authors and books and sort that information.

Student Directions

1.   Open a new workbook.

2.   Click the **Select All** button to highlight the entire worksheet.

3.   Find the *Formatting* toolbar. Click **View** on the Menu bar. Click ***Toolbars>*** and choose *Formatting*. Use this toolbar to choose the Times font and to set the font size at 14.

4.   Change the row height. Click **Format** on the Menu bar. Choose ***Row***. Choose *Height...* Set the height at .5 in./48 pixels.

5.   Select the first column, *Book Name*. Click **Format** on the Menu bar. Choose ***Column*** and then ***Width...*** Set the width at 3 in./288 pixels.

6.   Do the same for the second and third columns, *Author* and *Date Read*. Set the width at 2 in./192 pixels.

7.   Set the width for the fourth column, *Rating/10*. Set it at 1.5 in./144 pixels.

8.   Type in your column headings: *Book Name, Author, Date Read*, and *Rating/10*.

9.   Type in all your information. Check your work carefully.

10. Use the **Color Fill** button on *Formatting* toolbar to add color to your rows and columns.

11. Select the rows and titles with your data. Click **Data** on the Menu bar. Click ***Sort...*** Sort your data alphabetically in *ascending order* by book name.

12. Next, do a numerical sort in *descending order* by rating.

13. Save your list.

14. Print your work. First, click **File** and choose ***Print Preview*** to check your work.

Assessment Rubric

Strong **(3 Points)**	The student created and formatted the worksheet correctly.	The student entered all the text correctly.	The student printed the worksheet correctly.	The student fully understands the lesson objectives.
Effective **(2 Points)**	The student created and formatted most of the worksheet correctly.	The student entered most of the text correctly.	The student printed the worksheet.	The student understands the lesson objectives.
Emerging **(1 Point)**	The student created and formatted some of the worksheet correctly.	The student entered some of the text correctly.	The student attempted to print the worksheet.	The student somewhat understands the lesson objectives.
Not Yet **(0 Points)**	The student did not create and did not format the worksheet correctly.	The student did not enter the text correctly.	The student was unable to print the worksheet.	The student does not understand the lesson objectives.
Self Score				
Teacher Score				
Total Score				

Comments:

Literature Record

Lesson Description

Students create literature records and sort them alphabetically and numerically.

Content Standard

Students read fiction appropriate to grades 6–8.

Technology Skill

Students know how to sort lists in a workbook application.

Additional Technology Skills

- adding color to cells
- changing the font and the font size
- saving and printing work

Materials

- copy of book records
- student sample (filename: *lit.xls*)

Teacher Preparation

1. Print and review the student sample (filename: *lit.xls*).

2. You may want to design a recording sheet for students. Alternatively, you can copy the class roster and have students gather their data using the rosters.

Procedure

1. Explain to the students that they will be using a workbook (or spreadsheet) application to create a record of the books that all students in the class have read.

2. Open a new workbook (or spreadsheet file).

3. Explain to students that they will always need to think about the layout of worksheets (or spreadsheets) before they begin to create them. It is important for them to know what their worksheets are going to display, what the format will be, and what they will need to change to accommodate for the parameters of the assignment. Describe the information they will use for their worksheets. Students will be creating text-based columns for the student names and number-based columns to record the number of books read.

4. Review how to use the **Select All** button to change the font to Times and the font size to 14. Show students how to set the row height to .5 in./48 pixels. Also, set the column width to 1.5 in./144 pixels. (See page 27.) These settings will be the same for the entire worksheet.

Procedure (cont.)

5. Model entering column headings at the top of each column: *Name* and *Number of Books Read*.

6. Demonstrate to your students how to enter the text information for student names and how to enter numbers for the number of books read.

7. Show students how to use the **Fill Color** button on the *Formatting* toolbar to shade the rows and columns with color. (See page 14.) You may want students to align text in a particular way. Have them use the buttons on the *Formatting* toolbar to do so. (See pages 27 and 40.)

8. Show your students how to sort their data. They will learn to do an alphabetical sort. First, focus on highlighting the columns and rows involved. Since the title is not part of the sort, be sure to point out to the students that they will not want to highlight it. Next, click **Data** on the Menu bar and choose **Sort...** Show students how to select the direction of the sort to make it an *ascending sort* or a *descending sort*. Have students check to make sure they have the correct columns selected in the *Sort By* box. Share the student sample with the students (filename: *lit.xls*).

9. Show students how to sort data numerically as well.

10. You may want students to organize their data into charts. [Note: See the student sample.] If you wish to do this with students, provide them with detailed instructions.

11. Give students sufficient time to finish their projects. Provide materials (class rosters, recording sheets, and/or clipboards) to help them gather data.

12. When students are finished, have them save and print their work. First, have students click **File** on the Menu bar and choose **Print Preview** to check their work.

13. Have students share their work with you and their classmates.

14. Use the rubric provided on page 65 to assess this lesson.

Extension Idea

Ask students to include worksheets with the book names and number of students reading each book.

Student Directions

1. Open a new workbook.

2. Click the **Select All** button to highlight the entire worksheet.

3. Find the *Formatting* toolbar. Click **View** on the Menu bar. Click **Toolbars>** and choose *Formatting*. Use this toolbar to choose the Times font and to set the font size at 14.

4. Change the row height. Click **Format** on the Menu bar. Choose **Row**. Choose *Height…*

5. Set the height at .5 in./48 pixels.

6. Change the column width. Click **Format** on the Menu bar. Choose **Column**. Choose *Width…*

7. Set the width at 1.5 in./144 pixels.

8. Add titles to the top of each column. Type in the column headings: *Name* and *Number of Books Read*.

9. Type in all your information. Check your work carefully.

10. Add color to your rows and columns. Use the **Color Fill** button on the *Formatting* toolbar.

11. Select the rows and titles with your data. Click **Data** on the Menu bar. Choose **Sort…** Sort your data alphabetically in *ascending order* by name.

12. Next, do a numerical sort in *descending order*. Use this sort when printing.

13. Save your list.

14. Print your work. Before printing, click **File** and choose **Print Preview** to check your work.

Assessment Rubric

Strong (3 Points)	The student created and formatted the worksheet correctly.	The student entered all the text correctly.	The student printed the worksheet correctly.	The student fully understands the lesson objectives.
Effective (2 Points)	The student created and formatted most of the worksheet correctly.	The student entered most of the text correctly.	The student printed the worksheet.	The student understands the lesson objectives.
Emerging (1 Point)	The student created and formatted some of the worksheet correctly.	The student entered some of the text correctly.	The student attempted to print the worksheet.	The student somewhat understands the lesson objectives.
Not Yet (0 Points)	The student did not create and format the worksheet correctly.	The student did not enter the text correctly.	The student was unable to print the worksheet.	The student does not understand the lesson objectives.
Self Score				
Teacher Score				
Total Score				
Comments:				

A *Microsoft Excel* worksheet is a large grid made up of rows (horizontal) and columns (vertical) of cells. Words and numbers can be entered into the cells. *Excel* uses those words and numbers to perform mathematical calculations, make charts and graphs, and analyze data.

A data table organizes data so that it can be used in a variety of ways. To create a data table, users must know how to change row height and column width and know how to use the AutoSum feature to add up lists of numbers.

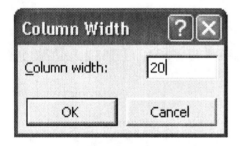

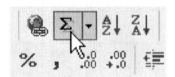

Quick Tip

To make a column or row wide enough to display all your text, double click on the separator between that column/row and the next column/row.

Step-by-Step Directions

Changing Row Height

1. Select the row or rows you are working with.

2. Click **Format** on the Menu bar. Choose *Row*. Choose *Height...*

3. Set the row height.

4. Click **OK**.

Changing Column Width

1. Select the column or columns you are working with.

2. Click **Format** on the Menu bar. Choose *Column*. Choose *Width...*

3. Set the column width.

4. Click **OK**.

Using the AutoSum Feature

1. Click the cell in which you want to add data. Type the data.

2. If you are entering values across a row, press the **Tab** key to move to the next column. Type the next number.

3. If you are entering values down a column, press the **Enter/Return** key to move to the next row. Type the next number.

4. Continue until you have entered all the necessary data.

5. Select the data.

6. Click the **AutoSum** button on the *Standard* toolbar. This will total your data.

Favorite Ice Cream Survey

Lesson Description

Students create tally sheets to survey what three ice cream flavors classmates prefer. They create data tables and use the AutoSum feature to total their results.

Content Standard

Students understand that information about objects or events can be collected.

Technology Skill

Students create data tables in a workbook application.

Additional Technology Skills

- adding color to cells
- adding borders to cells
- changing the font and the font size
- merging cells
- inserting and deleting rows
- saving and printing work

Materials

- student sample (filename: *ice.xls*)

Teacher Preparation

1. Print and review the student sample (filename: *ice.xls*).

2. You may want students to work independently, in pairs, or in small groups. Review the procedure and consider various groupings before you begin to teach the lesson.

Procedure

1. Explain to the students that they will be using a workbook (or spreadsheet) application to make tally sheets for a survey. They will make a list of the students in their class and tally their responses to a survey.

2. Open a new workbook (or spreadsheet file).

3. Explain to students that they will always need to think about the layout of worksheets before they create them. It is important for them to know what their worksheets are going to display, what the format will be, and what they will need to change to accommodate for the parameters of the assignment. Describe the information they will use for these worksheets. Students will be creating columns for the names of the students in the class and three columns for student survey responses. You can assign three flavors for all students to use (chocolate, vanilla, and strawberry), or you may want to do a quick presurvey to find out what flavors are popular.

4. Review how to use the **Select All** button to change the font to Times and the font size to 16. Encourage students to use the **Bold** button on the *Formatting* toolbar. (See page 27.)

Procedure (*cont.*)

5. Show students how to set the row height to .5 in./48 pixels and the column width to 1.5 in./144 pixels. (See page 66.)

6. Demonstrate how to enter the survey title, *Favorite Ice Cream*, into cell A1. Then, show them how to merge cells A1, B1, C1, and D1. (See page 40.)

7. Model adding the column headings: *Name*, *Chocolate*, *Vanilla*, and *Strawberry* to A2, B2, C2, and D2 cells.

8. Show your students how to enter students' names in the name column.

9. Show students how to insert and delete rows. They may need to do this as they enter data and check their work. Click **Insert** on the Menu bar and choose ***Rows***. Likewise, model deleting a row by clicking **Edit** on the Menu bar and choosing ***Delete***.

10. Students are now ready to create their tally sheets using their worksheet files. Give them sufficient time. Have them add the names and place borders around the cells they will be using. They can do this using the **Borders** button on the *Formatting* toolbar. (See page 29, step 10.) Once the tally sheets are ready, have your students print them.

11. Have students begin the survey. With each response, have students make a tally mark in the appropriate column next to the student's name.

12. The next step in the tally activity is transferring the tallied data to their data tables. Explain to students that to be able to total the responses they received, they will need to enter numbers, not text into the tables. Show them the difference between entering a *yes* response and a number response into cells. Have them add their data using the number *1*. For a *no* response, they need to enter a zero.

13. Now, the students are ready to learn how to use the AutoSum feature to total the responses in each column. Review the definition of a *sum*. Tell them that they want to know the sum of all the numbers in each column. Show them how to select all the cells in a particular row that contain data and click on the **AutoSum** button on the *Standard* toolbar. (See page 66.) Students will see the sum appear at the bottom of the column.

14. Give students sufficient time to finish their projects and encourage them to be creative with the cell fill colors. (See page 14.)

15. When students are finished, have them save, print, and share their work.

16. Use the rubric provided on page 70 to assess this lesson.

Extension Ideas

Students can survey different topics such as favorite pets, favorite theme parks, and favorite songs. Have students to make up their own survey questions.

Student Directions

1. Open a new workbook.

2. Click the **Select All** button to highlight the entire worksheet.

3. Find the *Formatting* and *Standard* toolbars. Click **View** on the Menu bar. Click **Toolbars>** and choose *Formatting* and *Standard*. Use the *Formatting* toolbar to choose the Times font and to set the font size at 16.

4. Set the row height at .5 in./48 pixels. Click **Format** on the Menu bar. Choose **Row** and then *Height…*

5. Set the width at 1.5 in./144 pixels. Click **Format** on the Menu bar. Choose **Column** and then *Width…*

6. Type the survey title, *Favorite Ice Cream*, in A1.

7. Merge cells A1, B1, C1, and D1. Highlight them and click **Format** on the Menu bar. Choose **Cells…** and click on the *Alignment* tab. Choose *Merge cells*.

8. Add the titles to the top of these columns. Type *Name* and the three flavors of ice cream (*Chocolate, Vanilla*, and *Strawberry*) in cells A2, B2, C2, and D2.

9. Type each student name in column A.

10. Use the **Borders** button on the *Formatting* toolbar to make a border around the survey.

11. Print your work. Survey your classmates.

12. Fill in your data on your worksheet. Enter a *yes* as a *1*. For a *no* response, enter a zero.

13. Add color to your rows and columns. Use the **Color Fill** button the *Formatting* toolbar.

14. Highlight the cells in a row that have the data. Click the **AutoSum** button on the *Standard* toolbar. The total will appear at the bottom of the row.

15. Save and print your work.

Assessment Rubric

Strong **(3 Points)**	The student created a *Favorite Ice Cream* survey tally sheet correctly.	The student formatted the worksheet, entered the data, and used the AutoSum feature correctly.	The student printed the survey tally sheet correctly.	The student fully understands the lesson objectives.
Effective **(2 Points)**	The student created a *Favorite Ice Cream* survey tally sheet.	The student formatted the worksheet, entered the data, and used the AutoSum feature.	The student printed the survey tally sheet.	The student understands most of the lesson objectives.
Emerging **(1 Point)**	The student attempted to create a *Favorite Ice Cream* survey tally sheet.	The student formatted the worksheet, entered data, and used the AutoSum feature with support.	The student attempted to print the survey tally sheet.	The student somewhat understands the lesson objectives.
Not Yet **(0 Points)**	The student did not create a *Favorite Ice Cream* survey tally sheet.	The student did not format the worksheet, enter the data, or use the AutoSum feature.	The student did not print the survey tally sheet.	The student does not understand the lesson objectives.
Self Score				
Teacher Score				
Total Score				

Comments:

Favorite Pizza Survey

Lesson Description

Students create tally sheets to survey what three pizza toppings classmates prefer. They create data tables and use the AutoSum feature to total their results.

Content Standard

Students understand that data can be organized in many ways.

Technology Skill

Students create data tables in a workbook application.

Additional Technology Skills

- adding color to cells
- adding borders to cells
- changing the font and the font size
- merging cells
- inserting and deleting rows
- saving and printing work

Materials

- student sample (filename: *pizza.xls*)

Teacher Preparation

1. Print and review the student sample (filename: *pizza.xls*).

2. You may want students to work independently, in pairs, or in small groups. Review the procedure and consider various groupings before you begin to teach the lesson.

Procedure

1. Explain to the students that they will be using a workbook application to make tally sheets for surveys they will be taking about favorite pizza toppings. They will make lists of the students in their class and tally their survey responses.

2. Open a new workbook (or spreadsheet file).

3. Explain to students that they will always need to think about the layout of worksheets (or spreadsheets) before they begin to create them. It is important for them to know what their worksheets are going to display, what the format will be, and what they will need to change to accommodate for the parameters of the assignment. Describe the information they will use for these worksheets. Students will be creating columns for the names of the students in the class, and four columns for student survey responses (one for each pizza flavor): cheese, pepperoni, vegetarian, and other. Discuss that they will use an "Other" category to be sure that they are not missing too many responses.

4. Review how to use the **Select All** button to change the font to Times and the font size to 16. Encourage students to use the **Bold** button on the *Formatting* toolbar. (See page 27.)

Procedure (*cont.*)

5. Show students how to set the row height to .35 in./33.6 pixels. Also, set the column width to 1.5 in./144 pixels. (See page 66.)

6. Model for your students how to enter the survey title, *Favorite Pizza Topping*, into cell A1. Then, show them how to merge cells A1, B1, C1, D1, and E1. (See page 40.)

7. Model adding the column headings: *Name*, *Cheese*, *Pepperoni*, *Vegetarian*, and *Other* to the A2, B2, C2, and D2.

8. Show your students how to enter the students' names in the name column. Provide them with name lists or give them the survey sheets with the names already added.

9. Show students how to insert and delete rows. They may need to do this as they enter data and check their work. Click **Insert** on the Menu bar and choose **Rows**. Likewise, model deleting a row by clicking **Edit** on the Menu bar and choosing **Delete**.

10. Have students create their tally sheets. Give them sufficient time to do so. Have students add the names and place borders around the cells they will be using. (See page 29, step 10.) Have them print their tally sheets.

11. Have the students ask each student in the class the survey question, "What is your favorite pizza topping?" With each response, have students make tally marks in the appropriate column.

12. Have students transfer the tallied data to data tables. To total the responses they received, they will need to enter a number, not text. Show them the difference between entering a *yes* response and a number *1* response into a cell. Have them add their data using the number *1*. For a *no* response, they need to enter a zero.

13. Now, students will use the **AutoSum** button to total the responses in each column. Review the definition of a *sum*. Tell students that they will need to know the sum of all the numbers in each column. Have them select all the cells in a particular row that contain data and click the **AutoSum** button on the **Standard** toolbar. Students will see that the sum appears at the bottom of the column.

14. Give students sufficient time to finish their projects and encourage them to be creative with the cell fill colors. (See page 14.)

15. When students are finished, have them save, print, and share their work.

16. Use the rubric provided on page 74 to assess this lesson.

Extension Ideas

Encourage students to choose their own survey topics. These topics can also relate to other areas of study.

Student Directions

1. Open a new workbook.

2. Click the **Select All** button to highlight the entire worksheet.

3. Find the *Standard* and *Formatting* toolbars. Click **View** on the Menu bar. Click **Toolbars>** and choose *Standard* and *Formatting*. Use the *Formatting* toolbar to change the font to Times and the font size to 16.

4. Change the row height to .35 in./33.6 pixels. Click **Format** on the Menu bar. Choose **Row** and then *Height…*

5. Change the column width to 1.5 in./144 pixels. Click **Format** on the Menu bar. Choose **Column** and then *Width…*

6. Type the survey title, *Favorite Pizza Topping*, into cell A1.

7. Merge cells A1, B1, C1, and D1. Select them and click **Format** on the Menu bar. Choose **Cells…** and click on the *Alignment* tab. Choose *Merge cells*.

8. Add the titles to the tops of the columns. Type *Name*, *Cheese*, *Pepperoni*, *Vegetarian*, and *Other* in cells A2, B2, C2, and D2.

9. Type each student's name in column A.

10. Make a border around the survey. Use the **Borders** button on the *Formatting* toolbar.

11. Print your work. Conduct the survey.

12. Enter your data into your worksheet. Enter a *yes* as a number *1*. For a *no* response, enter a zero.

13. Use the **Color Fill** button on the *Formatting* toolbar to add color to your rows and columns.

14. Highlight the cells in a row that have the data. Click the **AutoSum** button on the *Standard* toolbar. The total will appear at the bottom of the row.

15. Save and print your work. Click **File** and choose **Print Preview** first to check your work.

Assessment Rubric

Strong **(3 Points)**	The student created the *Favorite Pizza* survey tally sheet correctly.	The student formatted the worksheet, entered the data, and used the AutoSum feature correctly.	The student printed the survey tally sheet correctly.	The student fully understands the lesson objectives.
Effective **(2 Points)**	The student created the *Favorite Pizza* survey tally sheet.	The student formatted the worksheet, entered the data, and used the AutoSum feature.	The student printed the survey tally sheet.	The student understands most of the lesson objectives.
Emerging **(1 Point)**	The student attempted to create the *Favorite Pizza* survey tally sheet.	The student formatted the worksheet, entered the data, and used the AutoSum feature with support.	The student attempted to print the survey tally sheet.	The student somewhat understands the lesson objectives.
Not Yet **(0 Points)**	The student did not create the *Favorite Pizza* survey tally sheet.	The student did not format the worksheet, enter data, or use the AutoSum feature.	The student did not print the survey tally sheet.	The student does not understand the lesson objectives.
Self Score				
Teacher Score				
Total Score				

Comments:

Favorite Elective Survey

Lesson Description

Students create tally sheets to survey what class electives classmates prefer. They create data tables and apply sum equations to total their results.

Content Standard

Students interpret data in tables.

Technology Skill

Students create data tables in a workbook application.

Additional Technology Skills

- adding borders to cells
- adding colors to cells
- changing the font and the font size
- using aligning and text wrapping features
- merging cells
- applying a sum equation
- saving and printing work

Materials

- student sample (filename: *elect.xls*)

Teacher Preparation

1. Print and review the student sample (filename: *elect.xls*).

2. You may want students to work independently, in pairs, or in small groups. Review the procedure and consider various groupings before you begin to teach the lesson.

Procedure

1. Explain to the students that they will be using a workbook (or spreadsheet) application to make tally sheets for a survey they will be taking about favorite elective choices. They will make lists of the students in their class and tally their responses to the survey. Share the student sample (filename: *elect.xls*).

2. Open a new workbook (or spreadsheet file).

3. Explain to students that they will always need to think about the layout of worksheets (or spreadsheets) before they begin to create them. It is important for them to know what their worksheets are going to display, what the format will be, and what they will need to change to accommodate for the parameters of the assignment. Describe the information they will use for these worksheets. Students will be creating one column for the names of the students in the class and seven columns for student survey responses (one for each elective choice). The electives include *Home Economics*, *Wood Shop*, *Music*, *Art*, *Drama*, *Technology*, and *Other*. Explain that they will use the *Other* category to be sure that they are not missing too many responses.

Procedure (cont.)

4. Have students use the **Select All** button to change the font to Times, and the font size to 12. Have students set the row height at .25 in./24 pixels and the column width at 1.25 in./120 pixels. (See page 66.) These settings will be the same for the entire worksheet.

5. Show your students how to enter the survey title, *Favorite Elective Choice*, into cell A1. Then, show them how to merge cells A1 through H1. This can be done by selecting the cells and clicking **Format** on the Menu bar. Choose ***Cells…*** and click on the *Alignment* tab. Click on *Merge cells*. (See page 40.)

6. Model adding the column headings to A2 through H2. Then, show your students how to enter each student's name in the name columns.

7. Show students how to insert and delete rows. They may need to do this as they enter data. Click **Insert** on the Menu bar and choose ***Rows***. To delete a row, click **Edit** on the Menu bar and choose ***Delete***.

8. Have students create their tally sheets. Have them add the names and place borders around the cells they will be using by clicking the **Borders** button on the *Formatting* toolbar. (See page 29, step 10.) Have students print the tally sheets.

9. Now, have them ask each student in the class the survey question, "What is your favorite elective?" With each response, have students make tally marks in the appropriate columns.

10. Have students transfer the tallied data into the worksheets. Explain to students that to total the responses they collected, they will need to enter a number, not text. Show them the difference between entering a *yes* response and number *1* into cells. For *no* responses, they need to enter a zero. Have them add their data.

11. Now, the students are ready to learn how to enter a *formula* to total the responses in each column. Introduce the idea of a *sum equation* and the words that go along with it. Tell them that they will need to know the sum of all the numbers in each column. Have them place the cursor in the cell at the bottom of the column, click **Insert** on the Menu bar and choose ***Function…*** Students will have an option of picking a function. Show students how to pick the *SUM* function. Click **OK**. Then, check the function and click **OK** again. Students will see the sum appear at the bottom of the column.

12. Give students sufficient time to finish their projects. Encourage them to be creative with their cell fill colors. (See page 14.)

13. Have them save and print their work.

14. Use the rubric provided on page 78 to assess this lesson.

Extension Idea

Have students look online, in newspapers, or in magazines to find surveys. Have them share their findings.

Student Directions

1. Open a new workbook.

2. Click the **Select All** button to highlight the entire worksheet.

3. Find the *Formatting* toolbar. Click **View** on the Menu bar. Click **Toolbars>** and choose *Formatting*. Use this toolbar to change the font to Times and the font size to 12.

4. Change the row height to .25 in./24 pixels. Click **Format** on the Menu bar. Choose **Row** and then *Height...*

5. Change the column width to 1.25 in./120 pixels. Click **Format** on the Menu bar. Choose **Column** and then *Width...*

6. Type the survey title, *Favorite Elective*, into cell A1.

7. Merge cells A1 through H1. Select them and click **Format** on the Menu bar. Choose **Cells...** and click on the *Alignment* tab. Choose *Merge cells*.

8. Add the titles to the tops of the columns.

9. Type each student's name in the first column.

10. Use the **Borders** button on the *Formatting* toolbar. Make a border around the survey.

11. Print your work. Conduct your survey.

12. Fill in your data. Enter a *yes* as a number *1*. For a *no* response, enter a zero.

13. Use the **Color Fill** button on the *Formatting* toolbar to add color to your rows and columns.

14. Place the cursor in the cells at the bottom of each column. Click **Insert** and choose **Function...** Choose the *SUM* Function. Click **OK**. Check the equation and click **OK** again. This will add up your data. The sum will appear at the bottom of the column.

15. Save your work.

16. Print your work. Click **File** and check **Print Preview** first.

Assessment Rubric

Strong **(3 Points)**	The student created a *Favorite Elective* survey tally sheet correctly.	The student formatted the worksheet, entered data, and used a sum equation formula correctly.	The student printed the survey tally sheet correctly.	The student fully understands the lesson objectives.
Effective **(2 Points)**	The student created a *Favorite Elective* survey tally sheet.	The student formatted the worksheet, entered data, and used a sum equation formula.	The student printed the survey tally sheet.	The student understands most of the lesson objectives.
Emerging **(1 Point)**	The student attempted to create a *Favorite Elective* survey tally sheet.	The student formatted the worksheet, entered data, and used a sum equation formula with support.	The student attempted to print the survey tally sheet.	The student somewhat understands the lesson objectives.
Not Yet **(0 Points)**	The student did not create a *Favorite Elective* survey tally sheet.	The student did not format the worksheet, enter data, or use a sum equation formula.	The student did not print the survey tally sheet.	The student does not understand the lesson objectives.
Self Score				
Teacher Score				
Total Score				
Comments:				

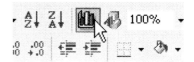
Using *Microsoft Excel*, you can not only enter and organize data, you can also use the data to create charts to visually display the data. It is often easier to analyze and present data in a chart or graph format.

Step-by-Step Directions

Creating a New Chart

1. Select the cells that contain the data you want to display in your chart. Include cells with row or column labels if you want the labels to be used in the chart.

2. Click the **Chart Wizard** button on the *Standard* toolbar.

3. At **Step 1**, select the type of chart you would like to create. You can click the *Press and Hold to View Sample* button to see how your data would look displayed in different types of charts. Click **Next >** once you have chosen a chart type.

4. At **Step 2**, click **Next >** as your data range should already be selected.

5. At **Step 3**, click in the *Chart title* box and type a chart title. Click in the *Category (X) axis* box and type a label for the horizontal axis of your chart. Click in the *Value (Y) axis* box to type a label for the vertical axis of your chart.

6. Click the different tabs to see some of the other options, such as adding a legend. Select each option to preview it and deselect any you do not want. Click **Next >** once you are finished.

7. In **Step 4**, select if you want your chart to be created as a new worksheet in your workbook or as an object within an existing worksheet.

8. Click **Finish** and your chart is instantly created.

Changing the Colors in a Chart

1. Click on the part of the chart you wish to change from one color to another. A Format Data Series dialog box will appear.

2. On a Macintosh: Click **View** and select the **Formatting Palette**. Click on the tab titled *Chart Colors, Lines, and Fills*.

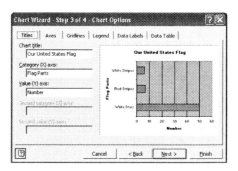

Quick Tip

The values in charts are linked to the cells in the worksheet you used to make the chart. If you click in a cell and change the value and then press **Enter/ Return** on your keyboard, the change will be reflected in the chart automatically.

Favorite Ice Cream Chart

Lesson Description

Students use their data tables from the *Favorite Ice Cream Survey* lesson (page 67) to create charts that graphically display the results of their surveys. They will work with bar charts or column charts.

Content Standard

Students understand that information can be represented in graphs.

Technology Skill

Students create charts in a workbook application.

Additional Technology Skills

- entering number and text data
- coloring the chart
- merging cells
- saving and printing work

Materials

- student sample (filename: *chart.xls*)

Teacher Preparation

1. Print and review the student sample (filename: *chart.xls*).

2. Make sure that students have access to their work from the *Favorite Ice Cream Survey* lesson.

3. Gather samples of bar/column charts, pie charts, and line charts to share with students.

Procedure

1. Explain to the students that they will be using a workbook (or spreadsheet) application to make a chart for the survey they took about favorite ice cream flavors.

2. Open a new workbook (or spreadsheet file).

3. Explain that there are three major chart types in *Excel*. They include a bar or column chart, a pie chart, and a line chart. Show them examples of each and discuss the differences between them.

- A *bar* or *column chart* represents number differences in data results. An example is the number of people choosing each flavor of ice cream.

- A *pie chart* represents the parts of the whole, such as how much of a week's allowance was spent in different ways. For this survey, the whole is the total number of students taking the survey.

- A *line chart* represents changes over time, such as weather and temperature changes over a month. Mention that the data they collected is not the type of data that would be used in a line chart.

Procedure (*cont.*)

4. Show students the student sample (filename: *chart.xls*). Explain to the students that they will work on bar/column charts and that they will use the results from their *Favorite Ice Cream* surveys.

5. Using the student sample (filename: *chart.xls*), show students how to use their data to create a new chart. Type the title, *Favorite Type of Ice Cream Survey*, in A1.

6. Then, show them how to merge cells A1 through D1. (See page 40.)

7. Model typing the column headings (*Type of Ice Cream*, *Vanilla*, *Chocolate*, and *Strawberry*) in cells A2–D2.

8. Model typing *Number of Students* in cell A3.

9. Show students how to use the data from their previous work to add data to these new charts.

10. When all data has been added, show students how to select the data so they can make a chart.

11. Click the **Chart Wizard** button on the *Standard* toolbar. This button will display the possible chart types that can be selected. Show students what they would need to select to create their column/bar charts.

12. Click **Next >**. The student's data range should already be selected in **Step 2**. Click **Next >**.

13. Model adding a chart title, an *X-axis* label, and a *Y-axis* label. Click **Next >**.

14. In **Step 4**, decide if you want the charts to be created in new worksheets in the workbooks or as objects within existing worksheets.

15. Click **Finish** and the charts are created.

16. Give students sufficient time to finish their projects. Encourage them to color their charts to make them easier to view. (See page 79.)

17. When students are finished, have them save and print their finished work. Remind them to click and check **Print Preview** first.

18. Use the rubric provided on page 83 to assess this lesson.

Extension Ideas

Have each student create a survey and do a quick count of the results of the survey question. After asking questions, they can each make a data table and then a chart to display the results. Place the printed charts together into a booklet or post the charts on a bulletin board for display.

Student Directions

1. Open a new workbook.

2. Type your title, *Favorite Type of Ice Cream Survey*.

3. Merge cells A1 through D1. Click **Format** on the Menu bar and choose **Cells...** Click on the *Alignment* tab and then on *Merge cells*.

4. Type the column headings, *Type of Ice Cream*, *Vanilla*, *Chocolate*, and *Strawberry* in cells A2, B2, C2, and D2.

5. Type *Number of Students* in cell A3.

6. Add the rest of your data to the worksheet.

7. Select your data so you can make a chart.

8. Find the *Standard* toolbar. Click **View** on the Menu bar. Choose **Toolbars>** and then *Standard*.

9. Click the **Chart Wizard** button on the *Standard* toolbar. You will see the possible chart types you can select for your data. Choose a **Column or Bar Chart**.

10. Click **Next >**. Your data should already be selected in **Step 2**. Click **Next >**.

11. Add a chart title. Add an *X-axis* and a *Y-axis* label. Click **Next >**.

12. Follow your teacher's directions for **Step 4**.

13. Click **Finish** and your chart will appear.

14. Change the colors on your chart. This makes your data easier to see.

15. When your chart is finished, save it.

16. Print your work. First, click **File** on the Menu bar. Choose **Print Preview** to check your work.

Assessment Rubric

Strong **(3 Points)**	The student created a chart and formatted it correctly.	The student changed colors on the chart.	The student printed the chart correctly.	The student fully understands the lesson objectives.
Effective **(2 Points)**	The student created a chart and formatted it with support.	The student changed colors on the chart with support.	The student printed the chart with support.	The student understands the lesson objectives.
Emerging **(1 Point)**	The student attempted to create a chart and format it.	The student attempted to change colors on the chart.	The student attempted to print the chart.	The student somewhat understands the lesson objectives.
Not Yet **(0 Points)**	The student did not create a chart or format it.	The student did not change colors on the chart.	The student did not print the chart.	The student does not understand the lesson objectives.
Self Score				
Teacher Score				
Total Score				

Comments:

Favorite Pizza Chart

Lesson Description

Students use their data tables from the *Favorite Pizza Survey* lesson (page 71) to create charts that graphically display the results of their surveys. They will work with bar/column charts.

Content Standard

Students construct bar graphs using data.

Technology Skill

Students create charts in a workbook application.

Additional Technology Skills

- entering number and text data
- coloring the chart
- merging cells
- saving and printing work

Materials

- student sample (filename: *favtop.xls*)

Teacher Preparation

1. Print and review the student sample (filename: *favtop.xls*).

2. Make sure that students have access to their work from the *Favorite Pizza Topping Survey* lesson.

3. Gather samples of bar/column charts, pie charts, and line charts to share with students.

Procedure

1. Explain to the students that they will be using a workbook application to make a chart for the survey they took about favorite pizza toppings.

2. Open a new workbook (or spreadsheet file).

3. Explain that there are three major chart types in *Excel*. They include a bar or column chart, a pie chart, and a line chart. Show them examples and discuss the differences between them.

- A *bar* or *column chart* represents number differences in data results. An example might be the number of people choosing each pizza topping.

- A *pie chart* represents the parts of the whole, such as how much of a week's allowance was spent in different ways. For the *Elective* survey, the whole would be the total number of students taking the survey or answering the question.

- A *line chart* represents changes over time, such as weather and temperature changes over a month. Mention that the data they collected is not the type of data that would be used in a line chart.

Procedure *(cont.)*

4. Show students the student sample (filename: *favtop.xls*). Explain to the students that they will work on bar/column charts and they will use the results from the *Favorite Pizza Topping* surveys.

5. Using the student sample (filename: *ice.xls*), show students how to use their data to create a new chart. Type the title, *Favorite Pizza Topping Survey*, in cell A1.

6. Then, show them how to merge cells A1 and B1. This can be done by selecting the cells and clicking **Format** on the Menu bar. Choose ***Cells...*** and click on the ***Alignment*** tab. Click on *Merge cells*.

7. Model typing the column headings (*Favorite Topping* and *Number Choosing)* in cells A2 and B2.

8. Model typing the topping choices in column A.

9. Show students how to use the data from their previous work to add data to this new chart.

10. When you are finished adding all data, show students how to select the data so they can make a chart.

11. Click the **Chart Wizard** button on the *Standard* toolbar. This button will display the possible chart types that can be selected. Show students what they want to select to create column/bar charts.

12. Click **Next >**. The student's data range should already be selected in *Step 2*. Click **Next >**.

13. Model adding a chart title, an *X-axis* label, and a *Y-axis* label. Click **Next >**.

14. In *Step 4*, decide if you want the charts to be created in new worksheets in the workbooks or as objects within existing worksheets.

15. Click **Finish** and your chart is created.

16. Give students sufficient time to finish their projects. Encourage them to color their charts to make them easier to view. (See page 79.)

17. When students are finished, have them save and print their finished work. First, have students click on **File** on the Menu bar and choose ***Print Preview*** to check their work.

18. Have students share their work with you and with their classmates.

19. Use the rubric provided on page 87 to assess this lesson.

Extension Ideas

Have students experiment with using this data to create different kinds of charts.

Student Directions

1.   Open a new workbook.

2.   Type your title, *Favorite Pizza Topping Survey*.

3.   Merge cells A1 and B1. Click **Format** on the Menu bar.
     Choose **Cells...** and click the *Alignment* tab. Click on
     Merge cells.

4.   Type column headings, *Favorite Topping* and *Number
     Choosing*, in cells A2 and B2.

5.   Type the topping choices in column A.

6.   Add all your data.

7.   Select your data so you can make a chart.

8.   Find the *Standard* toolbar. Click **View** on the Menu bar.
     Choose **Toolbars>** and then *Standard*.

9.   Click the **Chart Wizard** button on the *Standard* toolbar.
     You will see the possible chart types you can select for
     your data. Choose a **Column** or **Bar Chart**.

10. Click **Next >**. Your data should already be selected in
     Step 2. Click **Next >**.

11. Add a chart title. Add an *X-axis* and a *Y-axis* label.
     Click **Next >**.

12. Follow your teacher's directions in **Step 4**.

13. Click **Finish** and your chart is created.

14. Change the colors on your chart. This makes your data
     easier to see.

15. When your chart is finished, save your work.

16. Print your work. First, click **File** on the Menu bar.
     Choose **Print Preview** to check your work.

Assessment Rubric

Strong **(3 Points)**	The student created a chart and formatted it correctly.	The student changed the colors on the chart.	The student printed the chart correctly.	The student fully understands the lesson objectives.
Effective **(2 Points)**	The student created a chart and formatted it with support.	The student changed the colors on the chart with support.	The student printed the chart with support.	The student understands the lesson objectives.
Emerging **(1 Point)**	The student attempted to create a chart and format it.	The student attempted to changed the colors on the chart.	The student attempted to print the chart.	The student somewhat understands the lesson objectives.
Not Yet **(0 Points)**	The student did not create a chart and format it.	The student did not change the colors on the chart.	The student did not print the chart.	The student does not understand the lesson objectives.
Self Score				
Teacher Score				
Total Score				

Comments:

Favorite Elective Chart

Lesson Description

Students use their data tables from the *Favorite Elective Survey* lesson (page 75) to create charts that graphically display the results of their surveys. They will work with bar/column charts.

Content Standard

Students interpret data in tables.

Technology Skill

Students create charts in a workbook application.

Additional Technology Skills

- entering number and text data
- coloring the chart
- merging cells
- saving and printing work

Materials

- student sample (filename: *favelect.xls*)

Teacher Preparation

1. Print and review the student sample (filename: *favelect.xls*).

2. Make sure that students have access to their work from the *Favorite Elective Survey* lesson.

3. Gather samples of bar/column charts, pie charts, and line charts to share with students.

Procedure

1. Explain to the students that they will be using a workbook (or spreadsheet) application to make a chart for the survey they took about favorite school electives.

2. Open a new workbook (or spreadsheet file).

3. Explain that there are three major chart types in *Excel*. They include a bar or column chart, a pie chart, and a line chart. Show them examples and discuss the differences between them. Be sure that they understand the differences.

- A *bar or column chart* represents number differences in data results. An example might be the number of people choosing each elective.

- A *pie chart* represents the parts of the whole, such as how much of a week's allowance was spent in different ways. For the *Elective* survey, the whole would be the total number of students taking the survey or answering the question.

- A *line chart* represents changes over time, such as weather and temperature changes over a month. Mention that the data they collected is not the type of data that would be used in a line chart.

Procedure *(cont.)*

4. Show students the student sample (filename: *favelect.xls*). Explain to the students that they will work on bar/column charts and they will use the results from their *Favorite Elective* surveys.

5. Using the student sample (filename: *elect.xls)*, show students how to use their data to create a new chart. Type a title, *Favorite Elective Choice*, in cell A1.

6. Then, show them how to merge cells A1 through H1. (See page 40.)

7. Model typing the column headings.

8. Model typing *Name, Total Choosing,* and *Percent Choosing* in column A.

9. Show students how to use the data from their previous work to add data to this new chart. Ask students to determine the percent on their own.

10. When you are finished adding all data, show students how to select the data so they can make a chart.

11. Click the **Chart Wizard** button on the *Standard* toolbar. This button will display the possible chart types that can be selected. Show students what they need to select to create a Column/Bar Chart.

12. Click **Next >**. The student's data range should already be selected in **Step 2**. Click **Next >**.

13. Model adding a chart title, an *X-axis* label and a *Y-axis* label. Click **Next >**.

14. In **Step 4**, decide if you want the charts to be created in new worksheets in the workbooks or as objects within existing worksheets.

15. Click **Finish** and your chart is created.

16. Give students sufficient time to finish their projects. Encourage them to color their charts to make them easier to view. (See page 79.)

17. When students are finished, have them save and print their finished work. Have students click on **File** and choose **Print Preview** to check their work before printing.

18. Have students share their work with you and with their classmates.

19. Use the rubric provided on page 91 to assess this lesson.

Extension Ideas

Have each student create a survey and do a quick count of the results of the survey question. One example might be, "Did you eat dinner at home or did you eat dinner out more this week?" After asking the questions, have each student make a chart to display the results. Post the charts on a bulletin board or have them put them into a *PowerPoint* slide show to show on open house night.

Student Directions

1. Open a new workbook.

2. Type your title, *Favorite Elective Choice*.

3. Merge cells A1 through H1. Click **Format** on the Menu bar. Choose **Cells...** and click on the *Alignment* tab. Click on *Merge cells*.

4. Type the column headings.

5. Type *Name*, *Total Choosing*, and *Percent Choosing* in column A.

6. Add all your data. Figure out percentages and add those to the data.

7. Select your data so you can make a chart.

8. Find the *Standard* toolbar. Click **View** on the Menu bar. Choose **Toolbars>** and then *Standard*.

9. Click the **Chart Wizard** button on the *Standard* toolbar. You will see the possible chart types you can select for your data. Choose a **Column** or **Bar Chart**.

10. Click **Next >**. Your data should already be selected in **Step 2**. Click **Next >**.

11. Add a chart title. Add an *X-axis* and a *Y-axis* label. Click **Next >**.

12. Follow your teacher's directions in **Step 4**.

13. Click **Finish** and your chart is created.

14. Change the colors on your chart. This makes your data easier to see.

15. When your chart is finished, save it.

16. Print your work. First, click **File** and choose **Print Preview** to check your work.

Assessment Rubric

Strong (3 Points)	The student created a chart and formatted it correctly.	The student changed colors on the chart.	The student printed the chart correctly.	The student fully understands the lesson objectives.
Effective (2 Points)	The student created a chart and formatted it with support.	The student changed colors on the chart with support.	The student printed the chart with support.	The student understands the lesson objectives.
Emerging (1 Point)	The student attempted to create a chart and format it.	The student attempted to change colors on the chart.	The student attempted to print the chart.	The student somewhat understands the lesson objectives.
Not Yet (0 Points)	The student did not create a chart or format it.	The student did not change colors on the chart.	The student did not print the chart.	The student does not understand the lesson objectives.
Self Score				
Teacher Score				
Total Score				

Comments:

One of the first skills needed to use an *Excel* worksheet is entering values. *Values* are the numbers entered into cells. When it comes to formatting the numbers in cells, *Excel* makes it easy for the data to be automatically formatted depending on the format you have determined for the cell. For example, you can format cells so that data entered is automatically formatted with or without decimal points, or as money (with or without symbols), or as a date in any number of styles.

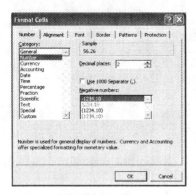

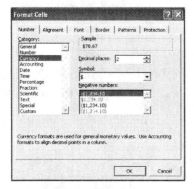

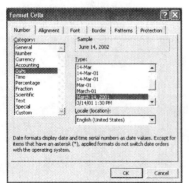

Step-by-Step Directions

Formatting Numbers

1. Select the cells that contain, or will contain, the numbers you want to format.

2. Click **Format** on the Menu bar.

3. Choose *Cells...*

4. Click on the *Number* tab on the Format Cells dialog box if it is not already at the forefront.

5. Under *Category*: click one of the choices depending on how you want to format numbers within your selected cells. For example:

   ● Select *Number* to change the number of places after a decimal point, to use a comma to separate thousands, and to format positive and negative numbers.

   ● Select *Currency* to add a dollar sign (or other currency symbol) to numbers as well as to determine the number of places after a decimal point and to format positive and negative numbers.

   ● Select *Date* to choose from a *Type* list on how you want dates to be displayed.

6. Click **OK**.

Quick Tip

To format all the cells in a column or row, simply click on the column letter at the top, or the row number at the left, and the entire column or row will be selected.

Helper Reward Chart

Lesson Description

Students work with number formats, decimals, and money. They create data tables to record their daily classroom helper activities and the class money they earned in return.

Content Standard

Students know that a number represents how many of something there is.

Technology Skill

Students enter and work with numbers in a workbook application.

Additional Technology Skills

- adding color to cells
- changing the font and font size
- entering data
- merging cells
- using the AutoSum feature
- saving and printing work

Materials

- student sample (filename: *helper.xls*)

Teacher Preparation

1. Print and review the student sample (filename: *helper.xls*)

2. Create a reward chart that students can use in your classroom.

3. You may want students to work independently, in pairs, or in small groups. You may even decide to teach this lesson to the whole group. Review the procedure and consider various groupings before you begin to teach the lesson.

Procedure

1. Explain to students that they will be learning about the difference between entering text and numbers in a workbook (or spreadsheet) application. They will try some examples and then make reward charts.

2. Open a new workbook (or spreadsheet file).

3. Review how to use the **Select All** button to change the font to Times and the font size to 12. Show students how to set the row height to .35 in./33.6 pixels and the column width to 2 in./192 pixels. These settings will be the same for the entire worksheet. (See page 27.)

4. Use the first worksheet (or spreadsheet) of the student sample (*Example Practice Sheet*) as a way to lead students through your modeling. Begin by entering the column headings: *Text*, *Numbers*, and *Decimals*, into cells A1, B1, and C1 respectively. Use the **Fill Color** button to choose a different color to add to the background of each heading. This will help to make each column more distinctive. (See page 14.)

Procedure (*cont.*)

5. Model selecting a cell or group of cells and click **Format** on the Menu bar to check or change the format of the cell. Show students how to choose **Cells...** and select the *Number* tab on the Format Cells dialog box.

6. Explain the difference between text and number values. Text cells are treated as text even when numbers are added. No mathematical functions can be performed with these cells. When the cell format is changed to numbers, the numbers can be treated mathematically. They can be added, sorted, averaged, etc. Experiment with text and number format entries as a group.

7. Next, explain to students how decimals are formatted. Show students how to select the number of decimal places they want to follow a decimal point and explain that the computer will round any numbers off to meet the requirements. You may want to have students try this setting. (See page 92.)

8. Show students that they can select the currency format setting. Explain the relationship to decimals. You may want to have students try this format setting also.

9. Lead students through the process of making a *Class Helper Reward Chart*. A blank *Helper Chart* is provided as the second worksheet in the student sample (filename: *helper.xls*). A completed chart is also included as a third worksheet. Personalize the chart for your own classroom needs.

10. Assign a dollar value to specific classroom chores and have students track their earnings each day. Format the chart cells for currency and enter the days of the week. Have students create their own charts, format their numbers, and keep a daily record of their chores. At the end of the week, have students use the AutoSum feature to figure out their total dollar amounts. (See page 66.)

11. Give students sufficient time to finish their projects.

12. Encourage them to be creative with the cell fill colors they choose. (See page 79.)

13. When students are finished, have them save their work.

14. Use the rubric provided on page 96 to assess this lesson.

Extension Idea

Have students create time lines with one column for the date and another column for the facts. If they enter facts and dates as they find them, they can sort the order of the time line by date when they are finished. The time can be entered by year or, if a more specific time difference is needed, one of the date formats can be selected. For younger students, a class activity time line helps them to remember what they have finished in class throughout the year. Include milestones, such as School Starts, Halloween Party, Holiday Concert, Spirit Week, or School Olympics.

Student Directions

1. Open a new workbook.

2. Click the **Select All** button to highlight the whole worksheet.

3. Find the *Standard* and *Formatting* toolbars.
   Click **View** on the Menu bar. Click **Toolbars>** and choose *Standard* and *Formatting*.

4. Use the *Formatting* toolbar to choose the Times font and to set the font size at 12.

5. Set the row height at .35 in./33.6 pixels. Click **Format** on the Menu bar. Choose **Row**. Choose *Height...*

6. Set the column width at 2 in./192 pixels. Click **Format** on the Menu bar. Choose **Column**. Choose *Width...*

7. Type the title, *Class Helper Reward Chart*, into cell A1.

8. Merge cells A1 through G1. Select them and click **Format** on the Menu bar, then **Cells...** On the *Alignment* tab, choose *Merge cells*.

9. Add the titles to the columns. In B2 through F2, type the days of the school week. In G2, type *Week Total*.

10. Type the helper list in column A.

11. Highlight columns B through G. Click **Format** on the Menu bar. Choose **Cells...** and then *Number*. Choose *Currency*.

12. Enter your data throughout the week.

13. Add color to your rows and columns. Use the **Color Fill** button on the *Formatting* toolbar.

14. At the end of the week, total your dollars. Use the **AutoSum** button on the *Standard* toolbar.

15. Save and print your work.

Assessment Rubric

Strong **(3 Points)**	The student formatted numbers in cells correctly.	The student used the AutoSum feature correctly.	The student printed a worksheet correctly.	The student fully understands the lesson objectives.
Effective **(2 Points)**	The student formatted numbers in cells.	The student used the AutoSum feature.	The student printed a worksheet.	The student understands the lesson objectives.
Emerging **(1 Point)**	The student attempted to format numbers in cells.	The student attempted to use the AutoSum feature.	The student attempted to print a worksheet.	The student somewhat understands the lesson objectives.
Not Yet **(0 Points)**	The student did not format numbers in cells.	The student did not use the AutoSum feature.	The student did not print a worksheet.	The student does not understand the lesson objectives.
Self Score				
Teacher Score				
Total Score				

Comments:

Weekend Schedule

Lesson Description

Students work with different number formats. They create a weekend schedule that includes dates, time, phone numbers, and dollar amounts.

Content Standard

Students understand that mathematical concepts can be represented symbolically.

Technology Skill

Students enter and work with numbers in a workbook application.

Additional Technology Skills

- adding borders
- adding color to cells
- changing font and font size
- entering data
- merging cells
- saving work

Materials

- student sample (filename: *wkend.xls*)

Teacher Preparation

1. Print and review the student sample (filename: *wkend.xls*).

2. You may want students to work independently, in pairs, or in small groups. Review the procedure and consider various groupings before you begin to teach the lesson.

Procedure

1. Explain to the students that they will be learning about the difference between entering text and numbers in a workbook (or spreadsheet) application. They will be designing ideal schedules for the weekend and will input both text and numbers.

2. Open a new workbook (or spreadsheet file).

3. Review how to use the **Select All** button to change the font to Times and the font size to 12. Show students how to set the row height to .5 in./48 pixels. These settings will be the same for the entire worksheet. (See page 27.)

4. Use the first worksheet of the student sample (*Weekend Schedule*) as a way to lead students through your modeling. Begin by entering the title, *Dream Weekend Schedule*, in cell A1.

5. Then, show students how to merge cells A1 through F1. (See page 40.)

Procedure (cont.)

6. Model typing column headings in cells A2 through F2. Have students manually adjust the column width to allow room for the text or numbers. Show students how to do this by selecting the column and manually moving it out to a desired width.

7. Now, enter some sample data. Type a date, time, an ideal weekend activity, a friend whom you might like to do the activity with, the friend's phone number, and the cost of the activity.

8. Place a border around the cells. Use the **Borders** button on the *Formatting* toolbar. (See page 29.)

9. Model selecting a group of cells and then click **Format** on the Menu bar to check or change the format of the cell. Show students how to choose *Cells...* and click the *Number* tab on the Format Cells dialog box. (See page 92.)

10. Each column might require students to choose different categories. There are categories for date, time, and currency. The *Special* category can be used for phone numbers. Show students how to select a format for each category.

11. To save from adding the dollar sign when money amounts are entered, show students that they can select the currency format setting. Explain the relationship to decimals.

12. Show students how to use the **Fill Color** button on the *Formatting* toolbar. (See page 14.)

13. You may want students to align text in a certain way. Use the buttons on the *Formatting* toolbar. (See page 40.)

14. Lead students through the process of making a *Dream Weekend Schedule*. A blank schedule is provided as the first worksheet in the student sample. A sample schedule is also included as a second worksheet. Personalize the sample for your own classroom needs.

15. Give students sufficient time to finish their projects. Encourage them to be creative with the cell fill colors they choose. (See page 14.)

16. When students are finished, have them save their work. [Note: If you have students print their work, keep in mind that private phone numbers may be included on the schedule.]

17. Use the rubric provided on page 100 to assess this lesson.

Extension Idea

Have students create time lines with one column for the date and another column for the facts. If they enter facts and dates as they find them, they can sort the order of the timeline by date when they are finished. The time can be entered by year or, if a more specific time difference is needed, one of the date formats can be selected. Have students research different topics like early man, European explorers, or colonizing the Americas. Then, students can combine the information and make one all-inclusive time chart.

Student Directions

1. Open a new workbook.

2. Click the **Select All** button to highlight the entire worksheet.

3. Find the *Formatting* toolbar. Click **View** on the Menu bar. Click **Toolbars>** and choose *Formatting*. Use this toolbar to choose the Times font and to set the font size at 12.

4. Set the row height at .5 in./48 pixels. Click **Format** on the Menu bar. Choose **Row** and then *Height...*

5. Type the title, *Dream Weekend Schedule*, into cell A1.

6. Merge cells A1 through F1. Select them and click **Format** on the Menu bar. Choose **Cells...** Click the *Alignment* tab and choose *Merge cells*.

7. Add column headings in cells A2 through F2. Change the column width to fit the text.

8. Type your data.

9. Highlight the columns for phone number and cost of the activity.

10. Click **Format** on the Menu bar. Click **Cells...** and choose **Number**. Then, choose the right category.

11. Select your format.

12. Place a border around the cells. Use the **Borders** button on the *Formatting* toolbar.

13. Add color to your rows and columns. Use the **Color Fill** button on the *Formatting* toolbar.

14. Save your work.

Assessment Rubric

Strong **(3 Points)**	The student formatted numbers in cells correctly.	The student added color to rows and columns correctly.	The student added a border correctly.	The student fully understands the lesson objectives.
Effective **(2 Points)**	The student formatted numbers in cells.	The student added color to rows and columns.	The student added a border.	The student understands the lesson objectives.
Emerging **(1 Point)**	The student attempted to format numbers in cells.	The student attempted to add color to rows and columns.	The student attempted to add a border.	The student somewhat understands the lesson objectives.
Not Yet **(0 Points)**	The student did not format numbers in cells.	The student did not add color to rows and columns.	The student did not add a border.	The student does not understand the lesson objectives.
Self Score				
Teacher Score				
Total Score				

Comments:

Income and Expense Chart

Lesson Description

Students work with number formats, decimals, money, and dates. They create a data table to record income and expenses each week.

Content Standard

Students add rational numbers.

Technology Skill

Students enter and work with numbers in a workbook application.

Additional Technology Skills

- adding borders
- adding color to cells
- entering data
- using the AutoSum feature
- saving and printing work

Materials

- student sample (filename: *expense.xls*)

Teacher Preparation

1. Print and review the student sample (filename: *expense.xls*).

2. You may want students to work independently, in pairs, or in small groups. Review the procedure and consider various groupings before you begin to teach the lesson.

Procedure

1. Explain to the students that they will be learning about entering numbers in a workbook (or spreadsheet) application. They will make income and expense charts.

2. Open a new workbook (or spreadsheet file).

3. Review how to use the **Select All** button to change the font to Times, size 12. Show students how to set the row height to . 3 in./28.8 pixels and the column width to 2 in./192 pixels. These settings will be the same for the entire worksheet. (See page 27.)

4. Begin by entering the title (*Your Name and Income)*, in cell A1 and the subtitle, *Income*, in cell A2.

5. Then, show them how to merge cells A1 through C1. Do the same for cells A2 through C2. (See page 40.)

6. Type the rest of the headings as shown in the *Blank Income* worksheet in the student sample (filename: *expense.xls*).

Procedure *(cont.)*

7. Now, you can enter some sample data. Type a date, category, and an amount for each entry.

8. Model selecting a group of cells and then click **Format** on the Menu bar to check or change the format of the cells. Show students how to choose *Cells...* and click the *Number* tab on the Format Cells dialog box. (See page 92.)

9. Each column might require you to choose a different category. There are categories for date and currency. Show students how to select a format for each category.

10. To save from adding the dollar sign when money amounts are entered, show students that they can select the currency format setting. Explain the relationship to decimals. You may want to have students try this setting.

11. Show students how to get a total amount in column C using the **AutoSum** button on the *Standard* toolbar. (See page 66.)

12. Place a border around the cells. Use the **Borders** button on the *Formatting* toolbar. (See page 29, step 10.)

13. Show students how to use the **Fill Color** button on the *Formatting* toolbar to shade the rows and columns with color. (See page 14.) You may want students to align text in a certain way. Use the buttons on the *Formatting* toolbar to do so. (See page 40.)

14. Lead students through the process of making both an income and expense chart. A blank income and expense chart are provided in the student sample (filename: *expense.xls*). Sample charts are also included. Personalize the sample for your own classroom needs.

15. Give students sufficient time to finish their projects.

16. Encourage them to be creative with the cell fill colors they choose. (See page 14.)

17. When students are finished, have them save their work.

18. Use the rubric provided on page 104 to assess this lesson.

Extension Idea

Create a list for students or have them come up with a list of five items that they would be interested in buying. Be specific. Then, have students comparative shop for the items. Have them create a chart that includes the name of the item, store name, web address for future reference, price, taxes, and shipping charges. When students think they have found the lowest prices for each item, they can record their results and compare their findings with one another.

Student Directions

1. Open a new workbook.

2. Click the **Select All** button to highlight the entire worksheet.

3. Find the *Standard* and *Formatting* toolbars. Click **View** on the Menu bar. Click **Toolbars>** and choose *Standard* and *Formatting*.

4. Use the *Formatting* toolbar to choose the Times font and to set the font size at 12.

5. Set the row height at .3 in./28.8 pixels. Click **Format** on the Menu bar. Choose **Row**. Choose *Height…*

6. Set the column width at 2 in./192 pixels. Click **Format** on the Menu bar. Choose **Column**. Choose *Width…*

7. Type the title (*Your Name and Income*), into cell A1. Type the subtitle, *Income,* into cell A2.

8. Merge cells A1 through C1. Select them and choose the **Format** menu. Choose **Cells…** and on the *Alignment* tab, choose *Merge cells*. Do the same for cells A2 through C2.

9. Add other headings for the income page.

10. Add your data.

11. Highlight each column. Click **Format** on the Menu bar. Choose **Cells…** and choose *Number*. Then, choose the right category.

12. Select your format.

13. Find your totals. Use the **AutoSum** button on the *Standard* toolbar.

14. Place a border around the cells. Use the **Borders** button on the *Formatting* toolbar.

15. Add color to your rows and columns. Use the **Color Fill** button on the *Formatting* toolbar.

16. Save your work and then follow the same steps for your expense sheet.

Assessment Rubric

Strong **(3 Points)**	The student formatted numbers in cells correctly.	The student added color to rows and columns correctly.	The student added a border correctly.	The student used the AutoSum feature correctly.	The student fully understands the lesson objectives.
Effective **(2 Points)**	The student formatted numbers in cells.	The student added color to rows and columns.	The student added a border.	The student used the AutoSum feature.	The student understands the lesson objectives.
Emerging **(1 Point)**	The student attempted to format numbers in cells.	The student attempted to add color to rows and columns.	The student attempted to add a border.	The student attempted to use the AutoSum feature correctly.	The student somewhat understands the lesson objectives.
Not Yet **(0 Points)**	The student did not format numbers in cells.	The student did not add color to rows and columns.	The student did not add a border.	The student did not use the AutoSum feature correctly.	The student does not understand the lesson objectives.
Self Score					
Teacher Score					
Total Score					

Comments:

Using *Microsoft Excel*, you can not only enter and organize data, but you can also use the data to create charts to visually display the data. It is often easier to analyze and present data in a graph format. Line graphs are particularly useful for illustrating changes in data over time.

Step-by-Step Directions

Creating a New Line Chart

1. Select the cells that contain the data you want to display in your line graph. Include cells with row or column labels if you want the labels to be used in the chart.

2. Click the **Chart Wizard** button on the *Standard* toolbar.

3. At **Step 1**, select *Line* from the list of chart types.

4. Click on one of the pictures to the right to select a *Chart sub-type*.

5. Click **Next >** once you have chosen a chart sub-type.

6. At **Step 2**, click **Next >** as your data range should already be selected.

7. At **Step 3**, click in the top text box and type a chart title. Click in the *Category (X) axis* text box and type a label for the horizontal axis of your chart. Click in the *Value (Y) axis* text box to type a label for the vertical axis of your chart.

8. Click the different tabs to explore some of the other options, such as adding a legend. You can select each option to preview it. Deselect it if you do not want it. Click **Next >** once you are finished.

9. In **Step 4**, select if you want your chart to be created on a new worksheet in your workbook or as an object within an existing worksheet.

10. Click **Finish** and your line chart is created.

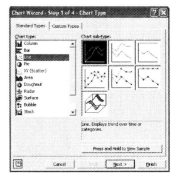

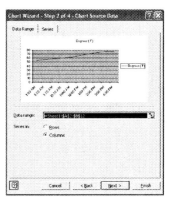

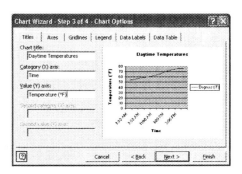

Quick Tip

To change the format of a chart, you can click on any part of the chart and a specific dialog box will appear that will allow you to make changes such as colors, fonts, and thickness of lines.

Spelling Test Record

Lesson Description

Students use the results from spelling tests to create a line chart to display their scores over time.

Content Standard

Students use letter-sound relationships to spell words.

Technology Skill

Students use a workbook application to create line charts.

Additional Technology Skills

- adding borders
- adding colors to rows and columns
- changing font and font size
- entering number and text data
- merging cells
- saving and printing work

Materials

- student sample (filename: *test.xls*)

Teacher Preparation

1. Print and review the student sample (filename: *test.xls*).

2. You may want students to work independently, in pairs, or in small groups. You may even want to complete this lesson as a whole class. Review the procedure and consider various groupings before you begin to teach the lesson.

Procedure

1. Tell students that they are going to make line charts. A line chart represents changes over time, such as temperature changes over a month.

2. Explain to students that they will make data tables and line charts to display the results of their weekly spelling tests. They will be recording their spelling test results every week on their data tables so that they can see how they are doing. [Note: This lesson can be used with scores from a series of tests in any subject.]

3. Open a new workbook (or spreadsheet file).

4. Review how to use the **Select All** button to change the font to Times and the font size to 12. Show students how to set the row height to .35 in./33.6 pixels. These settings will be the same for the entire worksheet. (See page 27.)

5. Tell students that column A will be set at 2 inches and the other columns, for the test scores, will be set at .5 in./48 pixels. (See page 27.) The number of columns for test scores will depend on the number of weeks you want your students to keep their records.

Procedure (*cont.*)

6. Show students how to add the title, *Spelling Test Scores*, in A1. Add the other titles to A2 and A3. Create titles that fit the needs of your students.

7. Then, show students how to merge cells A1 through B1. This can be done by selecting the cells and clicking **Format** on the Menu bar. Click **Cells...** and in the *Alignment* tab, click on *Merge cells*.

8. Once you have formatted your data table, show them how to enter their test score results. Explain that they can enter the test scores they already have, and then each week as they receive new scores, they can add the new scores to their data tables.

9. Show students how to add borders and cell fill colors to make their data easier to see. (See page 29, step 10 and page 14.)

10. Model selecting the data to make line charts. Show students where they will find the **Chart Wizard** button on the *Standard* toolbar. At *Step 1*, click *Line* from the list of chart types. Click a *Chart sub-type*. Select **Next>**.

11. At *Step 2*, your data range should already be selected. Click **Next>**. At *Step 3*, show students how to add a chart title and a label for the *X-axis* and *Y-axis*. Students may also decide to add legends, adjust the font size for their titles and the *X-axis* and *Y-axis* labels, and add or take away the grid markers.

12. In *Step 4*, decide if you want the charts to be created on a new worksheet in the workbooks or as an object within existing worksheets.

13. Click **Finish** and your chart is created.

14. Give students sufficient time to finish their projects. Encourage them to color their charts to make them easier to view. (See page 79.)

15. When students are finished, have them save and print their finished work. First, have students check their work by clicking **File** and choosing *Print Preview*.

16. Have students share their work with you and with their classmates.

17. Use the rubric provided on page 109 to assess this lesson.

Extension Ideas

Students can chart their timed math tests or any other regular test situation where it would be helpful for them to see their results over time. Have students analyze their results and use them to make plans for studying to improve their skills.

Many things in science show progress over time. Have students chart plant growth, rainfall in a month, or evaporation of water in a container. All these projects can generate data that can be represented with line graphs.

Student Directions

1. Open a new workbook.

2. Click the **Select All** button.

3. Find the *Standard* and *Formatting* toolbars. Click **View** on the Menu bar. Click **Toolbars>** and choose *Standard* and *Formatting*.

4. Use the *Formatting* toolbar to change the font to Times and set the font size at 12.

5. Change the row height to .35 in./33.6 pixels. Click **Format** on the Menu bar. Choose **Row** and then *Height…*

6. Change the width of column A to 2 in./192 pixels. Set the other columns at .5 inches. Click **Format** on the Menu bar. Choose **Column** and then *Width…*

7. Type the title, *Spelling Test Scores*, into cell A1. Type the other titles in A2 and A3.

8. Merge cells A1–B1. Select them and click **Format** on the Menu bar. Choose **Cells...** and on the *Alignment* tab, choose *Merge cells*. Now, add your data.

9. Place a border around the cells. Use the **Borders** button on the *Formatting* toolbar.

10. Add color to your rows and columns. Use the **Color Fill** button on the *Formatting* toolbar. Now, save your work.

11. Select your data and click the **Chart Wizard** button on the *Standard* toolbar.

12. At **Step 1**, click *Line* from the list of charts. Click a *Chart sub-type*. Select **Next>**.

13. At **Step 2**, your data range should already be selected. Click **Next>**.

14. At **Step 3**, add a chart title and a label for the *X-axis* and *Y-axis*. Follow your teacher's directions for **Step 4**.

15. Click **Finish** and your chart is created. Now, change the colors on your chart.

16. Save and print your chart.

Assessment Rubric

Strong **(3 Points)**	The student created a chart and formatted it correctly.	The student changed colors on the chart.	The student printed the chart correctly.	The student fully understands the lesson objectives.
Effective **(2 Points)**	The student created a chart and formatted it with support.	The student changed colors on the chart with support.	The student printed the chart with support.	The student understands the lesson objectives.
Emerging **(1 Point)**	The student attempted to create a chart and format it.	The student attempted to change colors on the chart.	The student attempted to print the chart.	The student somewhat understands the lesson objectives.
Not Yet **(0 Points)**	The student did not create a chart or format it.	The student did not change colors on the chart.	The student did not print the chart.	The student does not understand the lesson objectives.
Self Score				
Teacher Score				
Total Score				

Comments:

Temperature Averages Record

Lesson Description

Students research the local monthly average temperatures for one year and create a line chart to display their findings.

Content Standard

Students know that water changes from one state to another through various processes.

Technology Skill

Students use a workbook application to create line charts.

Additional Technology Skills

- adding borders
- adding colors to rows and columns
- changing font and font size
- entering number and text data
- merging cells
- navigating the Internet
- saving and printing work

Materials

- student sample (filename: *temp.xls*)

Teacher Preparation

1. Print and review the student sample (filename: *temp.xls*) for student reference.

2. You may want students to work independently, in pairs, or in small groups. You may even want to complete this lesson as a whole class. Review the procedure and consider various groupings before you begin to teach the lesson.

Procedure

1. Tell students that they are going to make line charts. A line chart represents changes over time, such as temperature changes over a year. Discuss the temperature average sample with them (filename: *temp.xls*).

2. Explain to the students that they will make data tables and line charts to display the average temperatures in their local area, or in another city.

3. Share the Weather Channel website with your students. Show them the different kinds of information they can find. Show them how to find specific temperatures or rainfall measurements for their chosen city.

4. Open a new workbook (or spreadsheet file).

5. Review how to use the **Select All** button to change the font to Times and the font size to 10. Show students how to set the row height to .35 in./33.6 pixels and the column width to .75 in./72 pixels. These settings will be the same for the entire worksheet. (See page 27.)

Procedure *(cont.)*

6. Show students how to add the title, *Temperature Averages for (your city),* in cell A1. Add the other titles to cells A2 and A3.

7. Then, show them how to merge cells A1 through C1. (See page 40.)

8. Once you have formatted the data table, show students how to enter their data. They may have recorded their data earlier by hand or saved it from the computer, or they can look it up on the computer and transfer the numbers immediately to their data tables. Make sure students check the accuracy of their data.

9. Show students how to add borders using the **Borders** button on the *Formatting* toolbar. (See page 29.) Have students add colors using the **Fill Color** button on the *Formatting* toolbar to make their data easier to see. (See page 14.)

10. Model how to select data to make a line chart. Show students where the **Chart Wizard** button is on the *Standard* toolbar. At **Step 1**, click *Line* from the list of chart types. Click a *Chart sub-type.* Select **Next>**.

11. At **Step 2**, your data range should already be selected. Click **Next>**.

12. At **Step 3**, show students how to add a chart title and a label for the *X-axis* and *Y-axis.* Students may also add legends, adjust the font size for their titles and the *X-axis* and *Y-axis* labels, and add or take away the grid markers.

13. In **Step 4**, decide if you want the charts to be created on a new worksheet in the workbooks or as an object within existing worksheets.

14. Click **Finish** and your chart is created.

15. Give students sufficient time to finish their projects. Encourage them to color their charts to make them easier to view. (See page 79.)

16. When students are finished, have them save and print their finished work. Before they print, have them check their work by clicking **File** and choosing **Print Preview**.

17. Use the rubric provided on page 113 to assess this lesson.

Extension Idea

Have students further explore the Weather Channel website. Challenge them to find information that is important to them and to make line charts to display the information. They might choose different locations, such as vacation spots. They may choose to chart rainfall or weather related to skin protection or air quality. Have them share their data tables and charts and explain the relevance of the information.

Student Directions

1. Open a new workbook.

2. Click the **Select All** button to highlight the entire worksheet.

3. Find the *Standard* and *Formatting* toolbars. Click **View** on the Menu bar. Click **Toolbars>** and choose *Standard* and *Formatting*.

4. Use the *Formatting* toolbar to change the font to Times and set the font size at 10.

5. Set the row height at .35 in./33.6 pixels. Click **Format** on the Menu bar. Click **Row**. Choose *Height...*

6. Set the column width at .75 in./72 pixels. Click **Format** on the Menu bar. Click **Column**. Choose *Width...*

7. Type the title, *Temperature Averages for (your city)*, into cell A1. Type the other titles in A2 and A3.

8. Merge cells A1 through C1. Select them and click **Format** on the Menu bar. Choose **Cells...** Click the *Alignment* tab and choose *Merge Cells*. Now, add your data.

9. Place a border around the cells. Click the **Borders** button on the *Formatting* toolbar.

10. Add color to your rows and columns. Use the **Color Fill** button on the *Formatting* toolbar. Now, save your work.

11. Select all data and click the **Chart Wizard** button on the *Standard* toolbar.

12. At **Step 1**, click *Line* from the list of chart types. Click a *Chart sub-type*. Click **Next>**.

13. At **Step 2**, your data range should already be selected. Click **Next>**.

14. At **Step 3**, add a chart title and a label for the *X-axis* and *Y-axis*.

15. Follow your teacher's directions for **Step 4**.

16. Click **Finish** and your chart is created. Now, change the colors on your chart.

17. Save and print your work.

Assessment Rubric

Strong (3 Points)	The student created a chart and formatted it correctly.	The student changed colors on the chart.	The student printed the chart correctly.	The student fully understands the lesson objectives.
Effective **(2 Points)**	The student created a chart and formatted it with support.	The student changed the colors on the chart with support.	The student printed the chart with support.	The student understands the lesson objectives.
Emerging **(1 Point)**	The student attempted to create a chart and format it.	The student attempted to change colors on the chart.	The student attempted to print the chart.	The student somewhat understands the lesson objectives.
Not Yet **(0 Points)**	The student did not create a chart or format it.	The student did not change colors on the chart.	The student did not print the chart.	The student does not understand the lesson objectives.
Self Score				
Teacher Score				
Total Score				

Comments:

Stock Prices Record

Lesson Description

Students research the price of a stock for a predetermined period and create a line chart to display their findings.

Content Standard

Students know various types of specialized economic institutions found in market economies.

Technology Skill

Students use a workbook application to create line charts.

Additional Technology Skills

- entering number and text data
- adding borders
- adding colors to rows and columns
- merging cells
- saving and printing work

Materials

- Newspaper or websites with stock market information
- student sample (filename: *stock.xls*)

Teacher Preparation

1. Print and review the student sample (filename: *stock.xls*) for student reference.

2. You may want students to work independently, in pairs, or in small groups. You may even want to complete this lesson as a whole class. Review the procedure and consider various groupings before you begin to teach the lesson.

Procedure

1. Tell students that they are going to make line charts. A line chart represents changes over time, such as temperature changes over a month. Explain to the students that they will make a data table and line chart to display the prices of a stock for a specific time.

2. Discuss where your students will find their stock prices. You can show them how to find a stock price in the newspaper or online. Show them the different kinds of information they can find.

3. Open a new workbook (or spreadsheet file).

4. Review how to use the **Select All** button to change the font to Times and the font size to 10. Show students how to set the row height to .25 in./24 pixels and the column width to 1.25 in./120 pixels. These settings will be the same for the entire worksheet. (See page 27.)

5. Show students how to add the title, *(company name) Stock Report (dates)*, in cell A1. Add the other titles to cells A2 and A3. Create titles that fit the needs of your students.

Procedure *(cont.)*

6. Then, show students how to merge cells A1 through D1. (See page 40.)

7. Once you have formatted your data table, show students how to enter their values.

8. Show students how to add borders using the **Borders** button on the *Formatting* toolbar. (See page 29.) Have students add colors using the **Fill Color** button on the *Formatting* toolbar to make their data easier to see. (See page 14.)

9. Model selecting the data to make a line chart. Show students where they will find the **Chart Wizard** button on the *Standard* toolbar. At **Step 1**, click *Line* from the list of chart types. Click a *Chart sub-type*. Click **Next >**.

10. At **Step 2**, your data range should already be selected. Click **Next >**. At **Step 3**, show students how to add a chart title and a label for the *X-axis* and *Y-axis*. Students may also decide to add legends, adjust the font size for their titles and the *X-axis* and *Y-axis* labels, and add or take away the grid markers.

11. In **Step 4**, decide if you want the charts to be created on new worksheets in the workbooks or as an object within existing worksheets.

12. Click **Finish** and your chart is created.

13. Give students sufficient time to finish their projects.

14. Encourage them to color their charts to make them easier to view. (See page 79.)

15. When students are finished, have them save and print their finished work.

16. Have students share their work with you and with their classmates.

17. Use the rubric provided on page 117 to assess this lesson.

Extension Idea

Give students a specific dollar amount to spend on no more than five stocks. Have them research stocks before they make their purchases. Have them follow their stocks for a specified time period, record their price data in data tables, and create line charts to display their results. At the end of the time period, students can compare their results. There are several options for creating a final data table and chart to compare students' earnings or losses, including final worth, stock with the greatest gain, or stock with the greatest loss.

Student Directions

1. Open a new workbook.

2. Click the **Select All** button to highlight the entire worksheet.

3. Find the *Standard* and *Formatting* toolbars. Click **View** on the Menu bar. Click **Toolbars>** and choose *Standard* and *Formatting*.

4. Use the *Formatting* toolbar to change the font to Times and set the font size at 10.

5. Change the row height to .25 in./24 pixels. Click **Format** on the Menu bar. Choose **Row**. Choose *Height...*

6. Change the column width to 1.25 in./120 pixels. Click **Format** on the Menu bar. Choose **Column.** Choose *Width...*

7. Type the title, *(company name) Stock Report (dates)*, into A1.

8. Type the other titles in A2 and A3.

9. Merge cells A1 through D1. Select them and click **Format** on the Menu bar. Choose **Cells...** Click on the *Alignment* tab and choose *Merge cells*. Now, add your data.

10. Place a border around the cells. Use the **Borders** button on the *Formatting* toolbar.

11. Add color to your rows and columns. Use the **Color Fill** button on the *Formatting* toolbar. Now, save your work.

12. Highlight all your data. Click the **Chart Wizard** button on the *Standard* toolbar. At **Step 1**, click *Line* from the list of chart types. Click a *Chart sub-type*. Select **Next >**.

13. At **Step 2**, your data range should already be selected. Click **Next >**. **Step 3**, add a chart title and label the *X-axis* and *Y-axis*.

14. Follow your teacher's directions for **Step 4**.

15. Click **Finish** and your chart is created.

16. Change the colors on your chart to make your data easier to see.

17. When your chart is finished, save and print your work.

Assessment Rubric

Strong **(3 Points)**	The student created a line chart and formatted it correctly.	The student changed colors on the chart.	The student printed the chart correctly.	The student fully understands the lesson objectives.
Effective **(2 Points)**	The student created a line chart and formatted it with support.	The student changed colors on the chart with support.	The student printed the chart with support.	The student understands the lesson objectives.
Emerging **(1 Point)**	The student attempted to create a line chart and format it.	The student attempted to change colors on the chart.	The student attempted to print the chart.	The student somewhat understands the lesson objectives.
Not Yet **(0 Points)**	The student did not create a line chart or format it.	The student did not change colors on the chart.	The student did not print the chart.	The student does not understand the lesson objectives.
Self Score				
Teacher Score				
Total Score				

Comments:

Using *Microsoft Excel*, you can not only enter and organize data, you can also use the data to create charts to visually display the data. It is often easier to analyze and present data in a graph format. Pie charts are particularly useful for illustrating percentages found in data.

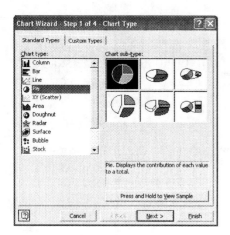

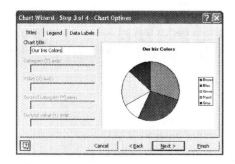

Step-by-Step Directions

Creating a New Pie Chart

1. Select the cells that contain the data you want to display in your pie chart. Include cells with row or column labels if you want the labels to be used in the chart.

2. Click the **Chart Wizard** button on the *Standard* toolbar.

3. At ***Step 1***, select *Pie* from the list of chart types. Then, click to select a *Chart sub-type*.

4. Click **Next >** once you have chosen a pie chart sub-type.

5. At ***Step 2***, click **Next >** as your data range should already be selected.

6. At ***Step 3***, click in the *Chart title* text box and type a title for your pie chart.

7. Click the different tabs to explore some of the other options, such as adding a legend and labeling the pieces of pie with percentages, labels, or values. You can select each option to preview it and deselect it if you do not want it.

8. Click **Next >** once you are finished.

9. In ***Step 4***, select if you want your chart to be created on a new worksheet in your workbook or as an object within an existing worksheet.

10. Click **Finish** and your pie chart is created.

Quick Tip

Double click a piece of the pie chart to open the Format Data Series dialog box and change the color or fill effects for each piece of the pie chart.

Shoe Choice Chart

Lesson Description

Students participate in a survey about shoe choice and use the data to create pie charts.

Content Standard

Students understand that information about objects or events can be collected.

Technology Skill

Students use a workbook application to create pie charts.

Additional Technology Skills

- adding borders
- adding colors to rows and columns
- entering number and text data
- merging borders
- saving and printing work

Materials

- chart paper and marker
- student sample (filename: *shoe.xls*)

Teacher Preparation

1. Print and review the student sample (filename: *shoe.xls*).

2. You may want students to work independently, in pairs, or in small groups. You may even want to do the lesson as a whole group. Review the procedure and consider various groupings before you begin to teach the lesson.

Procedure

1. Tell students that they are going to make pie charts. A pie chart represents percentages found in data. Review the concept of percentages and provide students with simple examples to help them understand the concept.

2. Explain to students that they will make a data table and pie chart to display the results of a survey about shoe choice. Review what a survey is and how they are used.

3. Tell students that the survey question will be, *What type of shoes are you wearing today?* Most shoes fit into one of the following three categories: tie, Velcro, or slip-on.

4. Carry out the survey with students. Use a large piece of chart paper to record the survey results.

5. Open a new workbook (or spreadsheet file).

6. Show students how to setup a worksheet to display their results. Review how to use the **Select All** button when choosing font type and size, and for setting column widths and row heights. (See page 27.) Share the student sample (filename: *shoe.xls*) with students.

Procedure *(cont.)*

7. Model for students how to include a title such as *Shoe Type* and headings such as *Number of Students, Tie, Velcro,* and *Slip-On.*

8. Then, show them how to merge cells A1 through D1. [Note: This may be different if you use additional categories of shoes in your survey.] (See page 40.)

9. Show the students how to add the data total for each type of shoe.

10. Show students how to add borders using the **Borders** button on the *Formatting* toolbar. (See page 29.) Have students add colors using the **Fill Color** button on the *Formatting* toolbar to make their data easier to see. (See page 14.)

11. Inform students that they will be making pie charts using the results from the survey. Discuss why they will use pie charts for these projects. Bar or column charts represent number differences in data results, while pie charts show pieces for each response group. For this survey, the whole would be the total number of students taking the shoe survey. Each response group—Tie, Velcro, and Slip-On would be a piece of the pie. Show students the differences in charts in the two worksheets from the student sample.

12. Model selecting the data to make a pie chart. Show students where the **Chart Wizard** button is located on the *Standard* toolbar.

13. At **Step 1**, click *Pie* from the list of chart types. Click a *Chart sub-type*. Click **Next>**.

14. At **Step 2**, your data range should already be selected. Click **Next>**. At **Step 3**, show students how to add chart titles. Students may also decide to add legends, adjust the font size for their titles, and add or take away the grid markers.

15. In **Step 4**, decide if you want the charts to be created on new worksheets in the workbooks or as an object within existing worksheets.

16. Click **Finish** and your chart is created.

17. Give students sufficient time to finish their projects. Encourage them to color their charts to make them easier to view. (See page 79.)

18. When students are finished, have them save and print their finished work. Have students check their work first by using **Print Preview**.

19. Use the rubric provided on page 122 to assess this lesson.

Extension Ideas

Have each student also make a bar/column chart with the same data that he or she selected for the pie chart. Have students compare the two charts.

Have students write mathematical problems about sharing. Have them show their results in data tables and make pie graphs from the results.

Student Directions

1. Open a new workbook.

2. Click the **Select All** button.

3. Find the *Standard* and *Formatting* toolbars. Click **View** on the Menu bar. Click **Toolbars>** and choose *Standard* and *Formatting*.

4. Use the *Formatting* toolbar to change the font to Times and set the font size at 14.

5. Change the row height to .5 in./48 pixels. Click **Format** on the Menu bar. Choose **Row**. Choose *Height…*

6. Change the column width to 2.5 in./240 pixels. Click **Format** on the Menu bar. Choose **Column**. Choose *Width…*

7. Type the title, *What Type of Shoe Are You Wearing Today?*, into cell A1. Type the other titles and headings.

8. Merge cells in the first row. Select the rows and click **Format** on the Menu bar. Choose **Cells…** and click on the *Alignment* tab. Choose *Merge cells*.

9. Now, add your data.

10. Place a border around the cells. Use the **Borders** button on the *Formatting* toolbar. Now, save your work.

11. Highlight all your data. Click the **Chart Wizard** button on the *Standard* toolbar.

12. At **Step 1**, click *Pie* from the list of chart types. Click a *Chart sub-type*. Select **Next>**.

13. At **Step 2**, your data range should already be selected. Click **Next>**.

14. At **Step 3**, add a chart title. Follow your teacher's directions for **Step 4**.

15. Click **Finish**. Your chart is created. Now, change the colors on your chart.

16. When your chart is finished, save it and print it.

Assessment Rubric

Strong **(3 Points)**	The student created a pie chart and formatted it correctly.	The student correctly changed colors on the pie chart.	The student printed the pie chart correctly.	The student fully understands the lesson objectives.
Effective **(2 Points)**	The student created a pie chart and formatted it with support.	The student changed colors on the pie chart with support.	The student printed the pie chart with support.	The student understands the lesson objectives.
Emerging **(1 Point)**	The student attempted to create a pie chart and format it.	The student attempted to change colors on the pie chart.	The student attempted to print the pie chart.	The student somewhat understands the lesson objectives.
Not Yet **(0 Points)**	The student did not create a pie chart or format it.	The student did not change colors on the pie chart.	The student did not print the pie chart.	The student does not understand the lesson objectives.
Self Score				
Teacher Score				
Total Score				

Comments:

Recess Activity Chart

Lesson Description

Students participate in a survey about what they like to do during recess and use the data to create pie charts.

Content Standard

Students understand that data can be organized in many ways.

Technology Skill

Students use a workbook application to create pie charts.

Additional Technology Skills

- adding borders
- adding colors to rows and columns
- entering number and text data
- merging cells
- saving and printing work

Materials

- chart paper and marker
- clipboards (optional)
- copies of class roster (optional)
- student sample (filename: *recess.xls*)

Teacher Preparation

1. Print and review the student sample (filename: *recess.xls*).

2. You may want students to work independently, in pairs, or in small groups. You may even want to do the lesson as a whole group. Review the procedure and consider various groupings before you begin to teach the lesson.

Procedure

1. Tell students that they are going to make pie charts. A pie chart represents percentages found in data. You may want to review the concept of percentages and provide students with simple examples to help them understand the concept.

2. Explain to students that they will make data tables and pie charts to display the results of a survey about what students do during recess. Review what surveys are and how they are used.

3. Tell students that the survey question will be, *What do you do during recess?* Determine the categories that are appropriate for your students. Write them on a piece of chart paper.

4. Have students carry out the survey. Give them paper and pencil. They should first write down the options for the survey. You might want to provide a checklist of students in the class so that they know they have asked each classmate.

5. Once the students have collected data, show them how to get started on the computer. Open a new workbook (or spreadsheet file).

Procedure (*cont.*)

6. Show the students how to setup a worksheet to display their results. Review how to use the **Select All** button for choosing font type and size and for setting column widths and row heights. (See page 14.) Share the student sample (filename: *recess.xls*).

7. Show students how to include a title such as *Favorite Recess Activities* and headings such as *Recess Activity* and *Number of Students*.

8. Then, show them how to merge cells A1 through D1. [Note: This may differ according to the number of additional categories of activities in your survey.] (See page 40.)

9. Show the students how to add the data totals for each activity.

10. Show students how to add borders using the **Borders** button on the *Formatting* toolbar. (See page 29.) Have students add colors using the **Fill Color** button on the *Formatting* toolbar. (See page 14.)

11. Inform students that they will be making pie charts using the results from the survey. Explain that a bar or column chart represents number differences in data results, while a pie chart shows pieces for each response group. For this survey, the whole would be the total number of students taking the survey. Each response would be a piece of the pie. Show the differences in the charts from the student sample (filename: *recess.xls*).

12. Model selecting the data to make a pie chart. Show students where they will find the **Chart Wizard** button on the *Standard* toolbar. At **Step 1**, click *Pie* from the list of chart types. Click a *Chart sub-type*. Select **Next>**.

13. At **Step 2**, your data range should already be selected. Click **Next>**. At **Step 3**, show students how to add a chart title. Students may also decide to add legends, adjust the font size for their titles, and add or take away the grid markers.

14. In **Step 4**, decide if you want the charts to be created on new worksheets in the workbooks or as an object within existing worksheets.

15. Click **Finish** and your chart is created.

16. Give students sufficient time to finish their projects. Encourage them to color their charts to make them easier to view. (See page 79.)

17. When students are finished, have them save and print their finished work. Have them check their work first by clicking on **File** and choosing **Print Preview**.

18. Use the rubric provided on page 126 to assess this lesson.

Extension Ideas

Have each student also make bar/column charts with the same data they selected for the pie charts. Have them compare the two charts.

Student Directions

1. Open a new workbook.

2. Click the **Select All** button.

3. Find the *Standard* and *Formatting* toolbars. Click **View** on the Menu bar. Click **Toolbars>** and choose *Standard* and *Formatting*.

4. Use the *Formatting* toolbar to change the font to Times and set the font size at 14.

5. Change the row height to .5 in./48 pixels. Click **Format** on the Menu bar. Choose **Row**. Choose *Height…*

6. Change the column width to 2 in./192 pixels. Click **Format** on the Menu bar. Choose **Column**. Choose *Width…*

7. Type the title, *Favorite Recess Activities*, in cell A1.

8. Type the other headings.

9. Merge cells in the first row. Select the rows and click **Format** on the Menu bar. Choose **Cells…** and click on the *Alignment* tab. Choose *Merge cells*. Now, add your data.

10. Place a border around the cells. Use the **Borders** button on the *Formatting* toolbar. Now, save your work.

11. Highlight all your data and click the **Chart Wizard** button on the *Standard* toolbar.

12. At **Step 1**, click *Pie* from the list of chart types. Click a *Chart sub-type*. Select **Next>**.

13. At **Step 2**, your data range should already be selected. Click **Next>**.

14. At **Step 3**, add a chart title. Follow your teacher's directions for **Step 4**.

15. Click **Finish**. Your chart is created.

16. Change the colors on your chart.

17. When your chart is finished, save it and print it.

Assessment Rubric

Strong **(3 Points)**	The student created a pie chart and formatted it correctly.	The student changed colors on the pie chart.	The student printed the pie chart correctly.	The student fully understands the lesson objectives.
Effective **(2 Points)**	The student created a pie chart and formatted it with support.	The student changed colors on the pie chart with support.	The student printed the pie chart with support.	The student understands the lesson objectives.
Emerging **(1 Point)**	The student attempted to create a pie chart and format it.	The student attempted to change colors on the pie chart.	The student attempted to print the pie chart.	The student somewhat understands the lesson objectives.
Not Yet **(0 Points)**	The student did not create a pie chart or format it.	The student did not change colors on the pie chart.	The student did not print the pie chart.	The student does not understand the lesson objectives.
Self Score				
Teacher Score				
Total Score				

Comments:

Food Nutrition Chart

Lesson Description

Students research calorie counts, focusing on carbohydrate, fat, and protein calorie content. They use the data to create pie charts.

Content Standard

Students know that making healthy food choices can be useful in attaining personal health goals.

Technology Skill

Students use a workbook application to create pie charts.

Additional Technology Skills

- adding borders
- adding color to rows and columns
- changing font and font size
- entering number and text data
- merging cells
- saving and printing work

Materials

- student sample (filename: *cal.xls*)
- food packaging showing calorie counts
- reference materials

Teacher Preparation

1. Print and review the student sample (filename: *cal.xls*).

2. Gather various print and/or online references for calculating calorie counts for food items.

Procedure

1. Explain to students that they will be using a workbook (or spreadsheet) application to make pie charts to display information for a particular kind of food.

2. Show students where they can find the calorie counts for food items using the samples you have brought in. Have them each research a particular food, focusing on its carbohydrate, fat, and protein calorie content. Provide resources and guidance during the research phase of this lesson.

3. Open a new workbook (or spreadsheet file).

4. Show the students how to setup worksheets to display their results. Review how to use the **Select All** button for choosing font type and size and for setting column widths and row heights. (See page 27.) Share the student sample provided (filename: *cal.xls*) with students.

5. Show students how to include a title and headings such as *Carbohydrate*, *Fat*, and *Protein*.

Procedure *(cont.)*

6. Then, show students how to merge cells A1 through D1. (See page 40.)

7. Show the students how to add the data totals.

8. Show students how to add borders. (See page 29.) Have students use the **Fill Color** button to make their data easier to see. (See page 14.)

9. Inform students that they will be making pie charts using the results from the research. Discuss why they will use pie charts. Bar or column charts represent number differences in data results, while pie charts show pieces for each response group. For this survey, the whole would be the total number of calories in the food. Each response group—Carbohydrate, Fat, and Protein would be a piece of the pie. Show students the differences in charts in the two worksheets from the student sample.

10. Model selecting the data to make a pie chart. Show students where they will find the **Chart Wizard** button on the *Standard* toolbar. At *Step 1*, click *Pie* from the list of chart types. Click a *Chart sub-type*. Select **Next>**.

11. At *Step 2*, your data range should already be selected. Click **Next>**. At *Step 3*, show students how to add chart titles. They may also add legends, adjust the font size for their titles, and add or take away the grid markers.

12. In *Step 4*, decide if you want the charts to be created on new worksheets in the workbooks or as an object within existing worksheets.

13. Click **Finish** and your chart is created.

14. Give students sufficient time to finish their projects. Encourage them to color their charts to make them easier to view. (See page 79.)

15. When students are finished, have them save and print their finished work. Have students check their work before printing by clicking on **File** on the Menu bar and choosing *Print Preview*.

16. Have students share their work with you and with their classmates.

17. Use the rubric provided on page 130 to assess this lesson.

Extension Ideas

Have students research historical events or geography facts and create social studies-related word problems about the events. Have them show their results in data tables and make pie graphs from the results. For example, students may compare the land area and water area of the United States of America.

Student Directions

1. Open a new workbook.

2. Click the **Select All** button to highlight the entire worksheet.

3. Find the *Standard* and *Formatting* toolbars. Click **View** on the Menu bar. Click **Toolbars>** and choose *Standard* and *Formatting*.

4. Use the *Formatting* toolbar to change the font to Times and set the font size at 12.

5. Change the row height .5 in./48 pixels. Click **Format** on the Menu bar. Click **Row**. Choose *Height…*

6. Change the column width to 2.5 in./240 pixels. Click **Format** on the Menu bar. Click **Column**. Choose *Width…*

7. Type the title into cell A1. Type the other titles and headings.

8. Merge cells in the first row. Select the cells and click **Format** on the Menu bar. Choose **Cells…** and click the *Alignment* tab. Choose *Merge cells*. Now, add your data.

9. Place a border around the cells. Use the **Borders** button on the *Formatting* toolbar. Now, save your work.

10. Highlight all data and click the **Chart Wizard** button on the *Standard* toolbar.

11. At **Step 1**, click *Pie* from the list of chart types. Click a *Chart sub-type*. Select **Next>**.

12. At **Step 2**, your data range should already be selected. Click **Next>**.

13. At **Step 3**, add a chart title.

14. Follow your teacher's directions for **Step 4**.

15. Click **Finish.** Your chart is created.

16. Change the colors on your chart.

17. When your chart is finished, save it and print it.

Assessment Rubric

Strong **(3 Points)**	The student created a pie chart and formatted it correctly.	The student changed colors on the pie chart.	The student printed the pie chart correctly.	The student fully understands the lesson objectives.
Effective **(2 Points)**	The student created a pie chart and formatted it with support.	The student changed colors on the pie chart with support.	The student printed the pie chart with support.	The student understands the lesson objectives.
Emerging **(1 Point)**	The student attempted to create a pie chart and format it.	The student attempted to change colors on the pie chart.	The student attempted to print the pie chart.	The student somewhat understands the lesson objectives.
Not Yet **(0 Points)**	The student did not create a pie chart or format it.	The student did not change colors on the pie chart.	The student did not print the pie chart.	The student does not understand the lesson objectives.
Self Score				
Teacher Score				
Total Score				

Comments:

A *Microsoft Excel* worksheet not only allows you to organize data, but also makes it easy to perform mathematical operations using the data. Formulas in *Excel* always begin with an equal sign (=) and usually include arithmetic operators such as + (add), – (subtract), * (multiply), and / (divide). You can create formulas using actual numbers such as =5+4, or cell references such as =C6–C5, or a combination of both such as =D6*2.

Step-by-Step Directions

Inserting a Function

1. Click the cell where you want to enter a formula.

2. Click **Insert** on the Menu bar.

3. Choose *Function...*

4. Find the category and function name you want. Click **OK**. [Note: There are short descriptions of each function at the bottom of the window.]

5. In the next box, check that the range of cells included in the function is correct. Click **OK**.

6. Your function will perform the chosen operation.

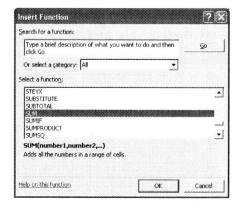

Constructing a Formula

1. Click the cell where you want to enter a formula.

2. Type **=** (equal sign) to signify that you are entering a formula in the cell.

3. Type the formula into the cell. If your formula references cell locations, you can either type the cell address or click on the cell and its address will appear in the formula.

4. Press **Enter/Return** on your keyboard when finished.

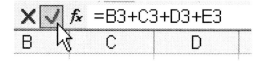

Quick Tip

If you want to copy a formula to adjacent cells in a row or column, select the formula and drag the fill handle (bottom, right corner of the cell) over the range you want to copy it to. If there are relative cell references (e.g., A1+A2 in column A), *Excel* will automatically adjust the formula accordingly (e.g., it would become B1+B2 if copied to column B).

Beginning Word Problems

Lesson Description

Students use formulas and calculations to solve beginning mathematical problems.

Content Standard

Students add whole numbers.

Technology Skill

Students use functions and formulas.

Additional Technology Skills

- adding color to cells
- changing font and font size
- entering number and text data
- merging cells
- saving and printing work

Materials

- student sample (filename: *calc.xls*)

Teacher Preparation

1. Print and review the student sample (filename: *calc.xls*).

2. You may want students to work independently, in pairs, or in small groups. You may even want to do the lesson as a whole group. Review the procedure and consider various groupings before you begin to teach the lesson.

3. Prepare a practice sheet with addition problems for students. Save it so that it is accessible to students. [Note: The sample file has two practice sheets that you may want to use.]

Procedure

1. Explain to the students that they will be using a workbook (or spreadsheet) application to help them solve mathematical problems. They will learn how to do addition on the computer.

2. Open a new workbook (or spreadsheet file).

3. Show students how to format the worksheet. Remind students that they will use the **Select All** button to make changes to the font type and size and for changing column widths and row heights. Show students how to set the font to Times and the font size to 14, the column width to .75 in./72 pixels, and the row height to .35 in./33.6 pixels. (See page 27.) Share the student sample (filename: *calc.xls*).

4. Explain how to do addition or calculate the *sum*. Finding the sum is the process of adding together different numbers.

Procedure (*cont.*)

5. In a separate window, open the practice worksheet you have prepared for calculation ideas. For example, discuss the equation 2 + 4 = 6.

6. Show students how to add numbers using formulas. Click in the cell in which you want to enter a formula. Have students click **Insert** on the Menu bar and choose *Function...*

7. Under *Function Category*, click *Math & Trig* and under *Function Name*, choose *SUM*. Click **OK**.

8. In the next box, it will show the range of cells used in this function. Point this out to students. Click **OK.**

9. Show students that the function has been performed and the answer has appeared in the cell.

10. When students have grasped the addition process, have them draft addition word problems. Decide how many word problems each student should write.

11. Show students the word problem example (filename: *calc.xls*) so they can use it as a reference for layout and data entry.

12. Give students sufficient time to finish their projects. Encourage them to shade the cell charts to make them easier to view by using **Fill Color** button on the *Formatting* toolbar. (See page 14.) They may also add borders using the **Borders** button. (See page 29.)

13. When students are finished, have them save their finished work. Show students how to prepare their documents for printing. Have them select the portions of the worksheets they want to print. They may not want to print their entire worksheets. Remind them to check **Print Preview** before printing to make sure that all the data they want included in the print job is showing.

14. Have students share their work with you and with their classmates.

15. Use the rubric provided on page 135 to assess this lesson.

Extension Idea

Have students make up word problems. They do not need to be math related. In social studies, for example, a student may draft a word problem related to Abraham Lincoln. *Abraham Lincoln was born in 1809 and he died in 1865. How old was he when he died? How old would he have been today?* Have students use real facts if they are available, or have them research online to find them. Students can challenge each other with their word problems.

Student Directions

1. Open a new workbook.

2. Click the **Select All** button.

3. Find the *Formatting* toolbar. Click **View** on the Menu bar. Choose **Toolbars>** and then *Formatting.* Use this toolbar to change the font to Times and to set the font size at 14.

4. Change the row height to .35 in./33.6 pixels. Click **Format** on the Menu bar. Choose **Row**. Choose *Height…*

5. Change the column width to .75 in./72 pixels. Click **Format** on the Menu bar. Choose **Column**. Choose *Width…*

6. Type a title in A1. It can be *Word Problem Sheet*. Add your name.

7. Merge cells A1 to C1. Select them and click **Format** on the Menu bar. Choose **Cells…** and click on the **Alignment** tab. Choose *Merge cells*.

8. Type your word problem in cell A2. Merge A2, B2, and C2.

9. Enter your facts below the word problem in Column A. Use one row for each fact.

10. Enter the number you will be using for each fact in Column B.

11. Click where you want the answer to go. Click **Insert** on the Menu bar, choose **Function . . .** and then choose *SUM*.

12. Check the cell range. Click **OK**.

13. Use the **Fill Color** button on the *Formatting* toolbar to add color to highlight your word problem and answer.

Assessment Rubric

Strong (3 Points)	The student formatted the worksheet and entered data correctly.	The student inserted a function correctly.	The student found the correct solutions to the word problems.	The student printed the worksheet correctly.	The student fully understands the lesson objectives.
Effective (2 Points)	The student formatted the worksheet and entered data with support.	The student inserted a function with support.	The student found solutions to the word problems.	The student printed the worksheet.	The student understands the lesson objectives.
Emerging (1 Point)	The student attempted to format the worksheet and enter data.	The student attempted to insert a function.	The student attempted to find solutions to the word problems.	The student attempted to print the worksheet.	The student somewhat understands the lesson objectives.
Not Yet (0 Points)	The student did not format the worksheet and enter data.	The student did not insert a function.	The student did not find solutions to the word problems.	The student did not print the worksheet.	The student does not understand the lesson objectives.
Self Score					
Teacher Score					
Total Score					

Comments:

Intermediate Word Problems

Lesson Description

Students use formulas and functions to solve intermediate mathematical problems.

Content Standard

Students multiply whole numbers.

Technology Skill

Students use functions and formulas.

Additional Technology Skills

- adding colors to cells
- adding borders
- entering number and text data
- saving and printing work

Materials

- student sample (filename: *word.xls*)

Teacher Preparation

1. Print and review the student sample (filename: *word.xls*).

2. You may want students to work independently, in pairs, or in small groups. You may even want to do the lesson as a whole group. Review the procedure and consider various groupings before you begin to teach the lesson.

3. Prepare a practice sheet with mathematical problems for students. Decide what kinds of calculations you want students to practice. Save it somewhere so that it is accessible to students. [Note: The sample file has two practice sheets that you may want to use.]

Procedure

1. Explain to students that they will be using a workbook (or spreadsheet) application to help them solve mathematical problems. They will learn how to do mathematical calculations on computers.

2. Open the practice sheet with word problems.

3. Review how to do addition or calculate the *sum*. Finding the sum is the processing of adding together different numbers.

4. Show students how to add numbers using formulas. Click in the cell in which you want to enter a formula. Click **Insert** on the Menu bar. Choose ***Function . . .***

5. Under *Function Category*, click *Math & Trig* and under *Function Name*, choose *SUM*. Click **OK**.

Procedure (*cont.*)

6. The next box will show the range of cells used in this function. Point this out to students. Click **OK**.

7. Show students that the function has been performed and the answer has appeared in the cell.

8. Explain to students that there is another way to perform calculations using *Excel*. Point out the **Formula Bar** at the top of your screen. If you cannot see it, you can select it by clicking **View** on the Menu bar and choosing **Formula Bar**.

9. Explain that students can write formulas that tell the computer how to compute numbers. Review the +, –, *, and / symbols and talk about how they are associated with addition, subtraction, multiplication, and division.

10. Review the use of cell labels (A1, A2, etc.). Write a simple addition formula. It might be as simple as =A1+A2. Tell students that formulas always start with an = sign.

11. Direct students to use their practice sheets. After students have practiced writing formulas, they can draft their own word problems. You can encourage students to create word problems that reflect the mathematical topics you are currently working on in class.

12. You may want to show students the word problem examples (filename: *word.xls*) so they can use them as a reference for layout and data entry.

13. You may want to use science topics or other math-related concepts for this lesson if you plan on using the samples provided.

14. Give students sufficient time to finish their projects. Encourage them to shade the cell charts to make them easier to view. They can use the **Fill Color** button on the *Formatting* toolbar. (See page 14.) They may also add borders using the **Borders** button. (See page 29.)

15. When students are finished, have them save their finished work. Show students how to prepare their documents for printing. Have them select the portions of the worksheets they want to print. They may not want to print their entire worksheets. Remind them to check **Print Preview** before printing to make sure that all the data they want included in the print job is showing.

16. Have students share their work with you and with their classmates.

17. Use the rubric provided on page 139 to assess this lesson.

Extension Idea

Have students makeup word problems related to something you are studying. For example, students may want to use a science topic and list the planets of our universe and the mass of each. With these facts, they may find the total mass of all the planets or find the difference in mass between the planets.

Student Directions

1. Open a workbook. Find the practice sheet.

2. Use functions and formulas to solve the problems.

3. Remember that each formula must start with an equal sign (=).

4. To use an addition function, click where you want the answer to go.

5. Click **Insert** on the Menu bar and choose ***Function . . .***

6. Pick the *SUM* function.

7. Check the cell range. Click **OK**.

8. Follow your teacher's directions to draft your own word problems.

9. Find the Formatting toolbar. Click **View** on the Menu bar. Click ***Toolbars>*** and choose *Formatting*.

10. Use the **Fill Color** and **Borders** buttons on the *Formatting* toolbar to make your worksheet easier to read.

11. Save your work.

12. Click **File** on the Menu bar. Choose ***Print Preview*** to check your page before printing.

13. Print your work.

Assessment Rubric

Strong (3 Points)	The student inserted a function or constructed a formula correctly.	The student found the correct solutions to the word problems.	The student printed the worksheet correctly.	The student fully understands the lesson objectives.
Effective (2 Points)	The student inserted a function or constructed a formula with support.	The student found solutions to the word problems.	The student printed the worksheet.	The student understands the lesson objectives.
Emerging (1 Point)	The student attempted to insert a function or construct a formula.	The student attempted to find solutions to the word problems.	The student attempted to print the worksheet.	The student somewhat understands the lesson objectives.
Not Yet (0 Points)	The student did not insert a function or construct a formula.	The student did not find solutions to the word problems.	The student did not print the worksheet.	The student does not understand the lesson objectives.
Self Score				
Teacher Score				
Total Score				

Comments:

Advanced Word Problems

Lesson Description

Students construct functions to solve advanced mathematical problems.

Content Standard

Students use computers for computation.

Technology Skill

Students use functions and formulas.

Additional Technology Skills

- adding borders
- adding color to cells
- entering number and text data
- saving and printing work

Materials

- student sample (filename: *advan.xls*)

Teacher Preparation

1. Print and review the student sample (filename: *advan.xls*).

2. Prepare a practice sheet with mathematical problems for students. Decide what kinds of calculations you want students to practice. Save this worksheet in a place that it is accessible to students. [Note: The sample file has two practice sheets that you may want to use.]

Procedure

1. Explain to the students that they will be using a workbook (or spreadsheet) application to help them solve mathematical problems. They will learn how to do addition, subtraction, multiplication, division, and power operations on computers.

2. Open the practice sheet with word problems.

3. Review how to do addition or calculate the *sum*. Finding the sum is the processing of adding together different numbers.

4. Review how to add numbers using formulas. Click in the cell in which you want to enter a formula. Have students click **Insert** on the Menu bar and choose **Function . . .**

5. Under *Function Category*, click *Math & Trig*. Under *Function Name*, choose *SUM*. Click **OK**.

6. The next box will show the range of cells used in this function. Point this out to students. Click **OK**.

Procedure (*cont.*)

7. Show students that the function has been performed and the answer has appeared in the cell.

8. Explain to students that there is another way to perform calculations using *Excel*. Point out the **Formula Bar** at the top of your screen. If you cannot see it, you can select it by clicking **View** on the Menu bar and choosing **Formula Bar**.

9. Explain to students that they can write formulas that tell the computer how to compute numbers. Review the +, –, *, /, and ^ symbols and talk about how they are associated with addition, subtraction, multiplication, division, and power operations.

10. Review the use of cell labels (A1, A2, etc.). Write a simple addition formula. It might be as simple as =A1+A2. Tell students that formulas always start with an = sign.

11. Show your students that they can also copy formulas from cell to cell. Show them how to select the formula and drag the fill handle (bottom, right corner of the cell) over the range you want to copy it to. If there are relative cell references (such as A1+A2 in column A), *Excel* will automatically adjust the formula accordingly (so it would become B1+B2 if copied to column B).

12. Help students get started by directing them to the practice sheet. After students have practiced writing formulas, they can draft their own word problems.

13. Encourage students to create word problems that reflect the mathematical topics you are currently working on in class. You may want to show students the word problem examples (filename: *advan.xls*) so they can use them as a reference for layout and data entry. [Note: You may want to use science topics or other math-related concepts for this lesson if you plan on using the samples provided.]

14. Give students sufficient time to finish the project. Encourage them to shade the cell charts to make them easier to view. They can use the **Fill Color** button. (See page 14.) They may also add borders using the **Borders** button. (See page 27.)

15. When students are finished, have them save their work. Show students how to prepare their documents for printing. Have them select the portions of the worksheets they want to print. They may not want to print their entire worksheets. Remind them to check **Print Preview** before printing to make sure that all the data they want included in the print job is showing.

16. Use the rubric provided on page 143 to assess this lesson.

Extension Idea

Have students create new practice sheets and trade them with classmates.

Student Directions

1. Open a new workbook. Find the practice sheet.

2. Use functions and formulas to solve the problems.

3. Remember that each formula must start with an equal sign (=).

4. To use an addition function, click where you want the answer to go. Click **Insert** on the Menu bar.

5. Choose **Function ...**

6. Pick the *SUM* function.

7. Check the cell range. Click **OK**.

8. Follow your teacher's directions to draft your own word problems.

9. Find the *Formatting* toolbar. Click **View** on the Menu bar. Click **Toolbars>** and choose *Formatting*.

10. Use the **Fill Colo**r and **Borders** buttons on the *Formatting* toolbar to make your worksheet easier to read.

11. Save your work.

12. Click **File** on the Menu bar. Choose **Print Preview** to check your page before printing.

13. Print your work.

Assessment Rubric

Strong **(3 Points)**	The student constructed a formula correctly.	The student found the correct solutions to the word problems.	The student printed the worksheet correctly.	The student fully understands the lesson objectives.
Effective **(2 Points)**	The student constructed a formula with support.	The student found solutions to the word problems.	The student printed the worksheet.	The student understands the lesson objectives.
Emerging **(1 Point)**	The student attempted to construct a formula.	The student attempted to find solutions to the word problems.	The student attempted to print the worksheet.	The student somewhat understands the lesson objectives.
Not Yet **(0 Points)**	The student did not construct a formula.	The student did not find solutions to the word problems.	The student did not print the worksheet.	The student does not understand the lesson objectives.
Self Score				
Teacher Score				
Total Score				

Comments:

Displaying and Printing
Summary

Microsoft Excel worksheets can become rather large and cumbersome as you fill more cells with data. As the worksheets become larger, it becomes more important to know how to print it so that it clearly displays the information you are trying to communicate. The Page Setup dialog box has all the important options for setting up your worksheet to print properly.

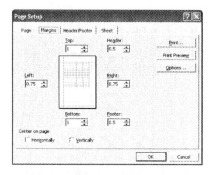

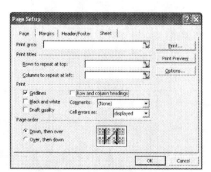

Step-by-Step Directions

Setting Page Orientation and Scale

1. Click **File** on the Menu bar. Choose **Page Setup...** Click the *Page* tab.

2. Under *Orientation*, click *Portrait* (vertical) or *Landscape* (horizontal).

3. Under **Scaling**, click *Adjust to* and change the **% to normal size** to the size you want. Alternatively, you can click *Fit to* and specify the number of pages wide and tall you want to print. Click **OK**.

Determining Margins and Centering on Page

1. Click **File** on the Menu bar. Choose **Page Setup...** Click the *Margins* tab.

2. Adjust margins by using the up and down arrows or by tying in the text boxes.

3. Under *Center on page*, click *Horizontally* to center from left to right. Click *Vertically* to center from top to bottom. Click both to center both ways on page. Click **OK**.

Setting Print Area and Printing Titles and Gridlines

1. Click **File** on the Menu bar. Choose **Page Setup...** Click the *Sheet* tab.

2. Click in the Print area text box. Highlight the cells in the worksheet that you want to print. The range of cells will appear in the textbox.

3. If you have labels that you want repeated on every printed page, click in the Print titles text boxes and highlight the *Rows to repeat at top* and then *Columns to repeat at left*.

4. Under *Print*, click the *Gridlines* box if you want the gridlines to appear on your printed worksheet. Click **OK**.

Quick Tip

Click **View** on the Menu bar and choose **Page Break Preview** to see where the page breaks occur before printing. You can click and drag the blue page break lines in the worksheet to change them.

Dinosaur Facts

Lesson Description

Students create research-based tables with information about dinosaurs. They experiment with different ways to display and print their work.

Content Standard

Students know that dinosaurs no longer exist.

Technology Skill

Students know how to use different display and printing options in a workbook application.

Additional Technology Skills

- changing the font and font size
- entering data
- formatting cells
- saving and printing work

Materials

- age-appropriate resources about dinosaurs
- student sample (filename: *dino.xls*)

Teacher Preparation

1. Print and review the student sample (filename: *dino.xls*).

2. You may want students to work independently, in pairs, or in small groups. You may even want to do the lesson as a whole group. Review the procedure and consider various groupings before you begin to teach the lesson.

3. Gather resources for the project, including books and online resources.

Procedure

1. Explain to the students that they will be using a workbook (or spreadsheet) application to create a table about dinosaur facts.

2. Describe the process for researching and recording dinosaur facts. In the student sample provided (filename: *dino.xls*), five dinosaurs were selected and each dinosaur's weight in pounds and length in feet were used. You can decide which dinosaurs will be studied and what statistics your students will collect. Have students collect their information.

3. Model opening and saving a new workbook (or spreadsheet file).

4. Format your worksheet to show your students how they will format their own worksheets. Students may need to use the **Select All** button to change the font or font size. You should also give directions for choosing column width and row height. (See page 27.)

Procedure *(cont.)*

5. Show students how to enter column titles into their cells and how to bold and center the titles in each cell. The titles in the example are *Dinosaur*, *Weight*, and *Length in Feet*.

6. Show students how to enter the data.

7. Give students sufficient time to finish their projects.

8. Have students save their work when they are finished.

9. Explain to students that once they are finished entering their data, they can then make choices about how their data will be displayed when printed onto paper. Model for students how to complete any of the options below. Decide which options are appropriate for the way in which students' data are organized.

    ● setting page orientation (landscape vs. portrait)

    ● changing margins

    ● printing titles or gridlines

    ● setting print area

10. Show students how to prepare their documents for printing. Remind them to click **File** on the Menu bar and choose *Print Preview* to check their work before printing to make sure that all the data they want included in the print job are showing.

11. Give students time to choose how their data will look when printed.

12. Have students save and print their work.

13. Have students share their work with you and with their classmates.

14. Use the rubric provided on page 148 to assess this lesson.

Extension Idea

Have students collect data on other animal groups from areas such as the rain forest, the Arctic, and the desert. You may want to have students compare size and weight. Other characteristics can also be compared. Have them add photos to their findings as well. Students can figure out which group has the longest, heaviest, tallest, and/or fastest animals and make awards for these categories.

Student Directions

1. Open a new workbook.

2. Format your worksheet. Follow your teacher's directions.

3. Use the **Select All** button to highlight the whole worksheet.

4. Find the *Formatting* toolbar. Click **View** on the Menu bar. Click **Toolbars>** and choose *Formatting*. Use this toolbar to change the font to Times and to set the font size at 14.

5. Change the column width to 2 in./192 pixels. Click **Format** on the Menu bar. Choose **Column**. Choose *Width…*

6. Change the row height to .25 in./24 pixels. Click **Format** on the Menu bar. Choose **Row**. Choose *Height…*

7. Enter your data. Save your work.

8. Decide how to display your work. How do you want your printed page to look?

9. You may want to change page orientation. Click **File** on the Menu bar. Choose **Page Setup…**

10. Click the *Page* tab and pick *Portrait* or *Landscape*.

11. You may want to change the margins. Click **File** on the Menu bar. Choose **Page Setup…**

12. Click the *Margins* tab.

13. You may want to print titles or gridlines. Click **File** on the Menu bar. Choose **Page Setup…**

14. Click the **Sheet** tab.

15. Check your work before printing. Click **File** on the Menu bar. Choose **Print Preview**.

16. Save and print your work.

Assessment Rubric

Strong **(3 Points)**	The student formatted data correctly.	The student independently made choices about how to display the data on the printed page.	The student printed the page correctly.	The student fully understands the lesson objectives.
Effective **(2 Points)**	The student formatted most of the data correctly.	The student made choices about how to display the data on the printed page.	The student printed the page.	The student understands the lesson objectives.
Emerging **(1 Point)**	The student attempted to format the data.	The student received support to make choices about how to display the data on the printed page.	The student printed the page with support.	The student somewhat understands the lesson objectives.
Not Yet **(0 Points)**	The student did not format the data.	The student did not make choices about how to display the data on the printed page.	The student did not print the page.	The student does not understand the lesson objectives.
Self Score				
Teacher Score				
Total Score				
Comments:				

Roller Coaster Facts

Lesson Description

Students create research-based tables with information about roller coasters. They experiment with different ways to display and print their work.

Content Standard

Students know that when a force is applied to an object, the object might speed up.

Technology Skill

Students know how to use different display and printing options in a workbook application.

Additional Technology Skills

- changing the font and font size
- entering data
- formatting cells
- saving and printing work

Materials

- age-appropriate resources about roller coasters
- student sample (filename: *roller.xls*)

Teacher Preparation

1. Print and review the student sample (filename: *roller.xls*).

2. You may want students to work independently, in pairs, or in small groups. Review the procedure and consider various groupings before you begin to teach the lesson.

3. Gather resources for the project, including books and online resources.

Procedure

1. Explain to the students that they will be using a workbook (or spreadsheet) application to create a table with facts about roller coasters.

2. Describe the process for researching and recording information about roller coasters. In the student sample provided (filename: *roller.xls*), five roller coasters were selected and the name, location, opening, and speed in miles per hour were used. You can decide which roller coasters will be studied and what statistics your students will collect. Have students collect their information.

3. Open a new workbook (or spreadsheet file).

4. Format your worksheet to show students how they will be formatting their worksheets. Students may need to use the **Select All** button to change the font or font size. You should also give directions for choosing column width and row height. (See page 27.)

Procedure (*cont.*)

5. Show students how to enter column titles into their cells, and bold and center the titles in each cell. (See page 40.) The titles in the example are *Amusement Park*, *Location*, *Date Opened*, and *Speed*.

6. Show students how to enter the data.

7. Give students sufficient time to finish their projects. You may want students to take the data and create tables. If so, make sure they know how to do so before they work independently.

8. Have students save their work when they are finished.

9. Explain to students that once they are finished entering their data, they can make choices about how their data are displayed when printed onto paper. Model for students how to complete any of the options below. Decide which options are appropriate for the way in which students' data is organized.

   ● setting page orientation (landscape vs. portrait)

   ● changing margins

   ● printing titles or gridlines

   ● setting print area

10. Show students how to prepare their documents for printing. Remind them to click **File** on the Menu bar and choose ***Print Preview*** to check their work before printing to make sure that all the data they want included in the print job are showing.

11. Give students time to choose how their data will look when printed.

12. Have students save and print their work.

13. Have students share their work with you and with their classmates.

14. Use the rubric provided on page 152 to assess this lesson.

Extension Idea

More facts about roller coasters are available. Have students select and research additional factors like type, design, height, drop, and length. Have them add pictures to their findings. Students can make posters and present awards for their favorite roller coasters.

Student Directions

1. Open a new workbook.

2. Format your worksheet. Follow your teacher's directions.

3. Use the **Select All** button to highlight the whole worksheet.

4. Find the *Formatting* toolbar. Click **View** on the Menu bar. Click **Toolbars>** and choose *Formatting*. Use this toolbar to change the font to Times and to set the font size at 14.

5. Change the column width to 2 in./192 pixels. Click **Format** on the Menu bar. Choose **Column**. Choose *Width...*

6. Change the row height to .25 in./24 pixels. Click **Format** on the Menu bar. Choose **Row**. Choose *Height...*

7. Enter your data. Save your work.

8. Decide how to display your work. How do you want your printed page to look?

9. You may want to change page orientation. Click **File** on the Menu bar. Choose **Page Setup...**

10. Click on the *Page* tab and pick *Portrait* or *Landscape*.

11. You may want to change the margins. Click **File** on the Menu bar. Choose **Page Setup...**

12. Click on the *Margins* tab.

13. You may want to print titles or gridlines. Click **File** on the Menu bar. Choose **Page Setup...**

14. Click on the *Sheet* tab.

15. Check your work before printing. Click **File** on the Menu bar. Choose **Print Preview**.

16. Save and print your work.

Assessment Rubric

Strong (3 Points)	The student formatted data correctly.	The student independently made choices about how to display the data on the printed page.	The student printed the page correctly.	The student fully understands the lesson objectives.
Effective (2 Points)	The student formatted most of the data correctly.	The student made choices about how to display the data on the printed page.	The student printed the page.	The student understands the lesson objectives.
Emerging (1 Point)	The student attempted to format the data.	The student received support to make choices about how to display the data on the printed page.	The student printed the page with support.	The student somewhat understands the lesson objectives.
Not Yet (0 Points)	The student did not format the data.	The student did not make choices about how to display the data on the printed page.	The student did not print the page.	The student does not understand the lesson objectives.
Self Score				
Teacher Score				
Total Score				

Comments:

Country Comparisons

Lesson Description

Students create research-based tables with information comparing countries. They experiment with different ways to display and print their work.

Content Standard

Students know regions within continents.

Technology Skill

Students know how to use different display and printing options in a workbook application.

Additional Technology Skills

- changing the font and font size
- entering data
- formatting cells
- conducting online research (optional)
- saving and printing work

Materials

- age-appropriate online resources about countries
- student sample (filename: *country.xls*)

Teacher Preparation

1. Print and review the student sample (filename: *country.xls*).

2. Locate several age-appropriate online resources for students to use during this lesson. Bookmark the sites so that students can access them when necessary.

Procedure

1. Explain to the students that they will be using a workbook (or spreadsheet) application to create tables comparing facts about different countries.

2. Share the online resources with your students. Discuss how to navigate each site and obtain the necessary information. Have students collect their information.

3. Model opening and saving a new workbook (or spreadsheet file).

4. Format your worksheet to show students how they will be formatting theirs. Students may need to use the **Select All** button to change the font or font size. You should also give directions for choosing column width and row height. (See page 27.)

5. Show students how to enter column titles into their cells, and how to bold and center the titles in each cell. (See page 40.)

Procedure *(cont.)*

6. Show students how to enter data.

7. Give students sufficient time to finish their projects. You may want students to create charts based on the data they collect. If so, review how to create a chart.

8. Have students save their work when they are finished.

9. Explain to students that once they are finished entering their data, they can then make choices about how their data are displayed when printed onto paper. Model for students how to complete any of the options below. Decide which options are appropriate for the way in which students' data are organized.

   ● setting page orientation (landscape vs. portrait)

   ● changing margins

   ● printing titles or gridlines

   ● setting print area

10. Show students how to prepare their documents for printing. Remind them to click **File** on the Menu bar and choose ***Print Preview*** to check their work before printing to make sure that all the data they want included in the print job are showing.

11. Give students time to choose how their data will look when printed.

12. Have students save and print their work.

13. Have students share their work with you and with their classmates.

14. Use the rubric provided on page 156 to assess this lesson.

Extension Idea

More facts about these countries are available. Have students select and research additional categories such as birth and death rates, literacy rates, or economic statistics. Have students add photos to their findings. Have students make posters comparing particular factors between the countries.

Student Directions

1. Open a new workbook.

2. Format your worksheet. Follow your teacher's directions.

3. Use the **Select All** button to highlight the whole worksheet.

4. Find the *Formatting* toolbar. Click **View** on the Menu bar. Click **Toolbars>** and choose *Formatting*. Use this toolbar to change the font to Times and to set the font size at 14.

5. Change the column width to 2 in./192 pixels. Click **Format** on the Menu bar. Choose **Column**. Choose *Width…*

6. Change the row height to .25 in./24 pixels. Click **Format** on the Menu bar. Choose **Row**. Choose *Height…*

7. Enter your data. Save your work.

8. Decide how to display your work. How do you want your printed page to look?

9. You may want to change page orientation. Click **File** on the Menu bar. Choose **Page Setup…**

10. Click on the *Page* tab and pick *Portrait* or *Landscape*.

11. You may want to change the margins. Click **File** on the Menu bar. Choose **Page Setup…**

12. Click on the *Margins* tab.

13. You may want to print titles or gridlines. Click **File** on the Menu bar. Choose **Page Setup…**

14. Click on the *Sheet* tab.

15. Check your work before printing. Click **File** on the Menu bar. Choose **Print Preview**.

16. Save and print your work.

Assessment Rubric

Strong **(3 Points)**	The student formatted data correctly.	The student independently made choices about how to display the data on the printed page.	The student printed the page correctly.	The student fully understands the lesson objectives.
Effective **(2 Points)**	The student formatted most of the data correctly.	The student made choices about how to display the data on the printed page.	The student printed the page.	The student understands the lesson objectives.
Emerging **(1 Point)**	The student attempted to format the data.	The student received support to make choices about how to display the data on the printed page.	The student printed the page with support.	The student somewhat understands the lesson objectives.
Not Yet **(0 Points)**	The student did not format the data.	The student did not make choices about how to display the data on the printed page.	The student did not print the page.	The student does not understand the lesson objectives.
Self Score				
Teacher Score				
Total Score				
Comments:				

Depending on the work you are doing, sheet tabs at the bottom of the screen are used to rename, move, delete, or add to. Having multiple worksheets makes it easy to have more than one related chart or list in the same file and to cross-reference them.

Additionally, when worksheets become filled with data, it often becomes helpful to freeze the columns and rows containing the labels so they are visible no matter where you scroll in your sheet.

One special feature of *Excel* that is useful to know, is how to add a built-in (custom) header or footer so that each page will show a title or page number or other information that will automatically appear when printed.

 Step-by-Step Directions

Working with Multiple Worksheets

1. Click on any worksheet tab to view its contents. If you do not see the worksheet tab you want, use the sheet tab scroll buttons to find it.

2. Click **Edit** on the Menu bar to find options to delete, move, or copy your sheet.

Freezing Panes

1. Click **View** on the Menu bar and choose either *Page break preview* or *Normal*.

2. To freeze the top horizontal pane, select the row below where you want the split to appear. To freeze the left vertical pane, select the column to the right of where you want the split to appear.

3. To freeze both the upper and left panes (both your row and column labels), click the cell below and to the right of where you want the split.

4. Click **Window** on the Menu bar. Choose *Freeze Panes*. To unfreeze the panes, click **Window** on the Menu bar and choose *Unfreeze Panes*.

Adding Headers and Footers

1. To select a built-in header and/or footer, click **View** on the Menu bar. Choose *Header and Footer...* Click **OK**. If you wish to customize a built-in header or footer or type one in, click either *Custom Header...* or *Custom Footer...*

2. Click in the *Left Section*, *Center Section*, or *Right Center* text boxes. Type your own text, or click one of the buttons such as *Insert Page Number*, *Insert Date*, *Insert Time*, or *Insert File Path*.

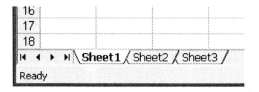

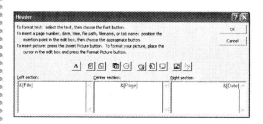

Quick Tip

To view multiple worksheets at the same time, open the workbooks you want to view. Click **Window** on the Menu bar and choose *Arrange* to tile them horizontally or vertically within the *Excel* window.

Family Celebrations

Lesson Description

Students conduct surveys about family celebrations enjoyed by classmates.

Content Standard

Students understand family heritage through celebrations.

Technology Skill

Students work with multiple worksheets and add headers and footers to their work.

Additional Technology Skills

- entering number and text data
- changing font and font size
- adding borders
- merging cells
- saving and printing work

Materials

- chart paper and marker
- books and other resources on families
- student sample (filename: *family.xls*)

Teacher Preparation

1. Print and review the student sample (filename: *family.xls*)

2. You may want students to work independently, in pairs, or in small groups. You may even want to do the lesson as a whole group. Review the procedure and consider various groupings before you begin to teach the lesson.

3. Gather resources for the project.

Procedure

1. Explain to the students that they will be conducting surveys about different favorite family celebrations represented in the class.

2. Use a variety of children's books to explore different family celebrations. Make a list of important celebrations on a piece of chart paper. Acknowledge that everyone's family enjoys different kinds of celebrations. [Note: It is important that you are sensitive to the different family backgrounds represented in your classroom. It is essential that you make the classroom climate accepting and tolerant so that students feel comfortable sharing their own family celebrations and heritage.]

3. Review with students what a survey is and how one conducts a survey. Discuss using a tally sheet to gather information. Explain to students that a tally sheet can be created using *Excel*.

4. Show students how to format a tally sheet. Open and save a workbook. Remind students how to use the **Select All** button to set the font to Times and the font size at 12.

Procedure *(cont.)*

5. Set the column width to 1.5 in./ 144 pixels and the row height to .4 in./38.4 pixels. (See page 27.)

6. Show your students how to set up the tally sheets. Type a title, such as *Family Celebrations Tally Sheet*, in cell A1. Change the title to a larger font.

7. As a class, decide on the celebrations that students will include in their surveys. Refer back to the ones listed earlier in the lesson. In the student sample provided, *Christmas*, *Ramadan*, *Hanukkah*, *Easter*, and *Passover* are used.

8. Show the students where to put categories for the survey. The celebration names can be typed in row 2, starting in cell B2. Type the student names into the cells in column A. Alternatively, you may simplify this lesson by providing students with an *Excel* template that already includes student names.

9. Model how to merge cells A1 through F1. This will vary depending on the number of categories included in the survey.

10. Borders for the cells are important. Model adding borders on the cells you are using so it will be easier to place tally results in the correct cell. (See page 29, step 10.)

11. Give students sufficient time to finish the tally sheets. Check that the tally sheets are correct before you ask students to print.

12. Have students perform the survey and tally their results.

13. Explain to students that they will copy their tally sheets and use the same format to organize the totals for the class tally. Show them how to copy their tally sheets to a new worksheet. Click **Edit** on the Menu bar and choose **Move or Copy Sheet...** Make sure the *Create a Copy* box is selected. This will duplicate the tally sheet. Click **OK**.

14. You can be creative about how to display the tally totals. Encourage your students to be creative as well. They might want to change fonts styles to help organize their work.

15. Show students how to add custom footers. Click **View** on the Menu bar and choose **Header and Footer...** Choose **Customize Footer...** In the Center section, type your name. Click **OK**.

16. Have students click **File** on the Menu bar and choose **Print Preview** to make sure the footer is correct.

17. Have them save and print their work.

18. Use the rubric provided on page 161 to assess this lesson.

Extension Ideas

Have students write stories that involve the different celebrations from the survey. Have them illustrate their stories.

Student Directions

1. Open a new workbook.

2. Use the **Select All** button to highlight the whole worksheet.

3. Find the *Formatting* toolbar. Click **View** on the Menu bar. Click ***Toolbars>*** and choose *Formatting*. Use this toolbar to change the font to Times and to set the font size at 12.

4. Change the column width to 1.5 in./144 pixels. Click **Format** on the Menu bar. Choose ***Column***. Choose *Width…*

5. Change the row height to .4 in./38.4 pixels. Click **Format** on the Menu bar. Choose ***Row***. Choose *Height…*

6. Type your title, *Family Celebrations Tally Sheet,* in cell A1.

7. Enter the categories for your survey. They can be typed in row 2. Start in cell B2.

8. Type the student names in column A.

9. Merge the cells in row 1. Select them and click **Format** on the Menu bar. Choose **Cells…** and click on the *Alignment* tab. Choose *Merge cells*.

10. Click on the **Borders** button on the *Formatting* toolbar to add borders to the cells you are using.

11. Print out a copy of your tally sheet. After you finish your survey, tally the results.

12. Copy your tally sheet to a new worksheet. Click **Edit** on the Menu bar. Choose ***Move or Copy Sheet…*** Make sure the *Create a Copy* box is selected. Display your totals.

13. Add your name as a footer. Click **View** on the Menu bar. Choose ***Header and Footer…*** and then *Customize Footer…*

14. In the Center section, type your name. Click **OK**.

15. Check your work. Click **File** on the Menu bar and choose ***Print Preview***. Save and print your work.

Assessment Rubric

Strong (3 Points)	The student formatted his or her survey tally sheet and worksheet and entered data correctly.	The student correctly added a custom footer.	The student printed his or her worksheet correctly.	The student fully understands the lesson objectives.
Effective (2 Points)	The student formatted the survey tally sheet and worksheet and entered the data.	The student added a custom footer.	The student printed his or her worksheet.	The student understands the lesson objectives.
Emerging (1 Point)	The student formatted some of the survey tally sheet and worksheet and entered some of the data.	The student attempted to add a custom footer.	The student attempted to print his or her worksheet.	The student somewhat understands the lesson objectives.
Not Yet (0 Points)	The student was unable to format the survey tally sheet and worksheet and enter data.	The student did not add a custom footer.	The student was unable to print his or her worksheet.	The student does not understand the lesson objectives.
Self Score				
Teacher Score				
Total Score				
Comments:				

City Population Statistics

Lesson Description

Students organize data on the population of nearby cities and towns.

Content Standard

Students know that the population of a city is the number of people who live in that city.

Technology Skill

Students work with multiple worksheets and add headers and footers to their work.

Additional Technology Skills

- adding borders
- changing font and font size
- entering data
- merging cells
- saving and printing work

Materials

- local maps and resources for researching population
- student sample (filename: *city.xls*)

Teacher Preparation

1. Print and review the student sample (filename: *city.xls*)

2. Decide on the local cities or towns that you want students to focus on in this lesson. Also, decide if you only want to focus on the current population figures. Another idea is to have students gather a few different figures over time for comparison.

3. Gather the necessary resources for this lesson. Find books or online resources for population statistics.

Procedure

1. Explain to the students that they will be researching the population statistics for nearby cities or towns. Make a list of the places you want the class to focus on in this lesson. Discuss their locations. Use a map or other resources to talk about where these places are located in relation to your town.

2. Open and save a workbook (or spreadsheet file).

3. Show students how to format the fact sheet. Remind students how to use the **Select All** button to make the format changes to their worksheet. Show students how to set the font to Times and the font size to 12. (See page 27.)

4. Set the column width to 1.5 in./144 pixels and the row height to .4 in./38.4 pixels. (See page 27.)

5. Type a title, such as *City Population Statistics*, in cell A1. You may want to change the title to a larger font.

Procedure (cont.)

6. Show the students where to place the city names. The names can be typed in row 2, starting in cell B2.

7. Are you focusing on population statistics from a single year or are you gathering statistics over time? If you are going to have more than one population number for each city, type those headings into the cells in column A.

8. Model how to merge cells A1 through F1. This will vary depending on the number of categories included in the fact sheet.

9. Borders for the cells are important. Model adding borders on the cells you are using so it will be easier to view data. (See page 29.)

10. Give students sufficient time to finish the fact sheet.

11. Show students how to copy their fact sheets to a new worksheet. Click **Edit** on the Menu bar and choose *Move or Copy Sheet...* Make sure the *Create a copy* box is selected. This will duplicate the fact sheet.

12. You can be creative about how to display the tally totals. Encourage your students to be creative as well. They may want to change font styles to help organize their work.

13. Show students how to add custom footers. They will do this before they print out their work. Click **View** on the Menu bar and choose *Header and Footer...* Choose *Customize Footer...* In the Center section, type your name. Click **OK**.

14. Have students click **File** on the Menu bar and choose *Print Preview* to make sure the footer is correct.

15. Give students time to complete this lesson.

16. Have students print their work.

17. Have students share their work with you and with their classmates.

18. Use the rubric provided on page 165 to assess this lesson.

Extension Ideas

Have students complete the same assignment but research state or country population statistics.

Student Directions

1. Open a new workbook.

2. Use the **Select All** button to highlight the whole worksheet.

3. Find the *Formatting* toolbar. Click **View** on the Menu bar. Click **Toolbars>** and choose *Formatting*. Use this toolbar to change the font to Times and to set the font size at 12.

4. Change the column width to 1.5 in./144 pixels. Click **Format** on the Menu bar. Choose **Column**. Choose *Width…*

5. Change the row height to .4 in./38.4 pixels. Click **Format** on the Menu bar. Choose **Row**. Choose *Height…*

6. Type your title in cell A1: *City Population Statistics*.

7. Enter the city names. They can be typed in row 2. Start in cell B2.

8. Did you find statistics for more than one year? Type the years in column A.

9. Merge the cells in row 1. Select them and click **Format** on the Menu bar. Choose **Cells…** and click on the *Alignment* tab. Choose *Merge cells*.

10. Use the **Borders** button on the *Formatting* toolbar to add borders to the cells you are using.

11. Copy your fact sheet to a new worksheet. Click **Edit** on the Menu bar. Choose **Move or Copy Sheet…** Make sure the *Create a Copy* box is selected.

12. Display your facts. Be creative. Save your work.

13. Add your name as a footer. Click **View** on the Menu bar and choose **Header and Footer…** Then, choose *Customize Footer…*

14. In the Center section, type your name. Click **OK**.

15. Check your work. Click **File** on the Menu bar and choose **Print Preview**. Save and print your work.

Assessment Rubric

Strong (3 Points)	The student formatted his or her fact sheet and worksheet and entered data correctly.	The student correctly added a custom footer.	The student printed his or her worksheets correctly.	The student fully understands the lesson objectives.
Effective (2 Points)	The student formatted the fact sheet and worksheet and entered the data.	The student added a custom footer.	The student printed his or her worksheets.	The student understands the lesson objectives.
Emerging (1 Point)	The student formatted some of the fact sheet and worksheet and entered some of the data.	The student attempted to add a custom footer.	The student attempted to print his or her worksheets.	The student somewhat understands the lesson objectives.
Not Yet (0 Points)	The student was unable to format the fact sheet and worksheet and enter data.	The student did not add a custom footer.	The student was unable to print his or her worksheets.	The student does not understand the lesson objectives.
Self Score				
Teacher Score				
Total Score				
Comments:				

Persuading an Audience

Lesson Description

Students organize information to be used in persuasive essays. Students add headers and footers to their work. They also freeze panes to help view their work.

Content Standard

Students address reader counterarguments.

Technology Skill

Students work with multiple worksheets, freeze panes, and add headers and footers to their work.

Additional Technology Skills

- adding borders
- changing font and font size
- entering number and text data
- merging cells

Materials

- resources related to topics explored in this lesson
- student sample (filename: *pers.xls*)

Teacher Preparation

1. Print and review the student sample (filename: *pers.xls*)

2. Gather resources for the project. You may want to find books or other print resources for student use. You may also want to preview related websites that students can use for this lesson.

3. Create a list of topics to start off the brainstorming session.

Procedure

1. Explain to the students that they will be picking topics to consider for persuasive essays. They will use *Excel* to organize their persuasive arguments and to explore any counterarguments.

2. Show students the list of topics that you have started. Ask them to offer ideas for additional topics. Add those ideas to the list.

3. Show students the resources you have collected for this lesson. Review how students may want to conduct research related to their topics.

4. Show students how to format worksheets (or spreadsheets). Open and save a workbook. Remind students how to use the **Select All** button to make necessary format changes. Change the font to Times and set the font size to 12. (See page 27.)

5. Set the column width to 2 in./192 pixels and the row height to .75 in./72 pixels. (See page 27.) [Note: You will want to show students how to manually change the column width once students start typing information into the cells.]

Procedure *(cont.)*

6. Type a title, such as *Elements of My Persuasive Argument*, in cell A1. You may want to change the title to a larger font. Model how to merge cells A1 through C1. (See page 40.)

7. Type three subheadings in row 2: *Issues*, *Pros*, and *Cons*.

8. Show the students where to type different categories (issues) related to this topic. They can be typed in column A.

9. It is important that students have several issues related to their topics. This will help necessitate the need to freeze panes, which will be taught later in the lesson.

10. Borders for the cells are important. Model adding borders, using the **Borders** button, on the cells you are using so it will be easier to view the information. (See page 29.)

11. Encourage students to be creative about how to display the information for their essays. They may want to change font styles to help organize their work.

12. Discuss the reason for freezing panes. Explain to students that when worksheets become filled with data, it often becomes helpful to freeze the columns or rows containing the labels so that they are visible no matter where they may scroll in their worksheets.

13. To freeze the top title and subtitles, select the row below where you want the split to appear. (This should be row 3.)

14. Click **Window** on the Menu bar. Choose *Freeze Panes*.

15. Show students how to add a custom footer. They will do this before they print out their work. Click **View** on the Menu bar and choose *Header and Footer...* Choose *Customize Footer...* In the Center section, type your name. Click **OK**.

16. Have students click **File** on the Menu bar and choose *Print Preview* to make sure the footer is correct.

17. Give students sufficient time to research their topics and organize the information.

18. Have students save and print their work.

19. Have students share their work with you and with their classmates.

20. Use the rubric provided on page 169 to assess this lesson.

Extension Idea

Have students write persuasive essays on the topics they researched and organized in this lesson.

Student Directions

1. Open a new workbook.

2. Use the **Select All** button to highlight the whole worksheet.

3. Find the *Formatting* toolbar. Click **View** on the Menu bar. Click **Toolbars>** and choose *Formatting*. Use this toolbar to change the font to Times and to set the font size at 12.

4. Change the column width to 2 in./192 pixels. Click **Format** on the Menu bar. Choose **Column** and then *Width…*

5. Change the row height to .75 in./72 pixels. Click **Format** on the Menu bar. Choose **Row** and then *Height…*

6. Type your title in cell A1: *Elements of My Persuasive Argument: (your topic)*. Type the three subheadings in row 2: *Issues, Pros,* and *Cons*.

7. Merge the cells in row 1. Select them and click **Format** on the Menu bar. Choose **Cells…** and click on the *Alignment* tab. Choose *Merge cells*.

8. Type the categories (issues) for your topic. They can be typed in column A.

9. Type the information under *Pros* and *Cons*.

10. Use the **Borders** button on the *Formatting* toolbar to add borders to the cells you are using.

11. Freeze the top rows, or panes. Select row 3. Make sure you are in **Normal** or **Page break preview**. Click **View** on the Menu bar. Click **Normal** or **Page break preview**. Click **Window** on the Menu bar. Click **Freeze Panes**.

12. Decide how to display your information. Be creative. Save your work.

13. Add your name as a footer. Click **View** on the Menu bar. Choose **Header and Footer…** Choose *Customize Footer…* In the Center section, type your name. Click **OK**.

14. Check your work. Click **File** on the Menu bar and choose **Print Preview**. Save and print your work.

Assessment Rubric

Strong **(3 Points)**	The student formatted his or her worksheet and entered data correctly.	The student correctly added a custom footer.	The student correctly froze the top rows.	The student fully understands the lesson objectives.
Effective **(2 Points)**	The student formatted the worksheet and entered the data.	The student added a custom footer.	The student asked for assistance to freeze the top rows.	The student understands the lesson objectives.
Emerging **(1 Point)**	The student formatted some of the worksheet and entered some of the data.	The student attempted to add a custom footer.	The student attempted to freeze the top rows.	The student somewhat understands the lesson objectives.
Not Yet **(0 Points)**	The student was unable to format the worksheet and enter data.	The student did not add a custom footer.	The student was unable to freeze the top rows.	The student does not understand the lesson objectives.
Self Score				
Teacher Score				
Total Score				
Comments:				

What Is Project-Based Learning?

Project-based learning (PBL) is an activity conducted over a certain period of time and resulting in a product, presentation, or performance (Moursund 1999). Most importantly, project-based learning focuses on a main problem or question. Students often work together and rely on their prior knowledge, skills, and experiences to find answers or discover solutions. The process by which the students come to discover an answer or solution is as important as the discovery itself.

Project-based learning differs from a more traditional classroom approach in a number of important ways. Perhaps most essential is the notion that students are actively engaged in their own learning. Rather than a teacher-directed classroom, project-based learning requires students to engage themselves in a quest to answer a question or solve a problem (TeacherVision 2007).

The following table highlights some of the potential differences between the project-based learning approach and a more teacher-centered, traditional classroom experience.

Project-Based Learning Classroom	Traditional Classroom
Student centered	Teacher centered
Constructivist and standards driven	Standards driven
Assessments based on criteria	Assessments based on norms
Focus on the depth of a topic	Focus on breadth of topics
Integrated thematic teaching	Teaching through single subjects
Focused on process and product	Focused on product only
Often use block scheduling	Instructional periods are short
Collaboration among teachers	Isolated teaching
Authentic assessment	Standardized assessment

Adapted from TeacherVision. 2007. Learner-centered vs. curriculum-centered teachers: Which one are you?

What Is Project-Based Learning? (cont.)

These four statements, which are further defined below, summarize project-based learning:

- Project-based learning is a natural fit with technology.
- Project-based learning integrates topics or skills from different subject areas and addresses standards requirements.
- Project-based learning is constructivist in nature.
- Project-based learning requires students to work collaboratively together.

Project-based learning is a natural fit with technology.

Project-based learning requires students to use various tools throughout the process of learning and discovering information. These tools can motivate learners to understand something in a new or different way. One such tool is technology. The use of technology for project-based learning activities allows students to conduct research, collaborate on projects, design presentations or finished products for others to view, or simply organize information in a visual way. In short, computers and other forms of technology allow students to do a task rather than to simply learn about a topic. This aspect of doing is a key tenet of project-based learning.

Project-based learning is more widespread today due to the increased availability of technology in the classroom. With a wealth of information available to students and teachers on the Internet, as well as easy-to-use software to organize, process, and present that information, project-based learning is more relevant and useful to the classroom today than ever before.

Project-based learning integrates topics or skills from different subject areas and addresses standards requirements.

Project-based learning activities are easily designed to address required content standards. Essential topics of study might incorporate multiple subjects within the curriculum. For example, social studies material can be covered while addressing research skills required in language arts. This need for integrating various subject areas can be addressed with project-based learning.

Likewise, technology-skill instruction can be easily integrated throughout a project. For example, the Internet is a wonderful tool for students to use to obtain information about a topic. Graphic organizers, word processors, or outlines can all be created with technology to organize and prepare information. Sharing findings with others, a critical component of project-based learning, is made easier with the use of technology as students can present information using slide shows, movies, Web pages, or graphic organizers.

What Is Project-Based Learning? (*cont.*)

Project-based learning is constructivist in nature.

A constructivist approach in education maintains that students build their own knowledge by starting with what they already know about a topic. In a project-based learning activity, students search for answers to questions, explore and investigate issues, and attempt to solve problems. They often start with their own prior knowledge and move forward from that point. As students research, investigate, discuss, and synthesize information, they begin to construct the knowledge they will eventually walk away with from the project. In the project-based learning approach, the teacher does not "feed" knowledge to students. Rather, the teacher guides and facilitates students through appropriate resources and processes and allows them to discover the knowledge.

Project-based learning requires students to work collaboratively together.

Project-based learning cannot work in a classroom with desks in rows and students isolated from each other. Collaboration and communication are essential to the project-based lesson, so one of the first things noticed in a project-based classroom are students working together in groups. The nature of project-based learning lends itself well to collaborative work as students learn from and help each other. For example, a common element of most project-based lessons is the need for students to find information to help them answer a question or solve a problem. Rather than have each student look for that information individually, they may work in small groups to search for the information. This way, students are not only helping and supporting each other, but they are also asking questions of each other, generating discussion, and contributing ideas. Working in groups helps foster a student's interpersonal skills, an essential skill necessary in both education and real-world settings.

What the Research Says

Educators who incorporate project-based learning techniques share anecdotal evidence of students relying on higher-level thinking skills, problem-solving strategies, and communication to further their learning. In addition, a solid body of research demonstrates the benefits of project-based learning. PBL has "generally been shown to be effective in increasing student motivation and in improving student problem-solving and higher-order thinking skills" (Stites 1998).

In a three-year study of two British secondary schools, in which one used a project-based approach and the other used a more traditional and direct instructional approach, there were significant differences in student understanding and in standardized achievement data in mathematics. The study was conducted by Jo Boaler (1999), an associate professor of

What the Research Says (*cont.*)

mathematics education at Stanford University, who found that students from the project-based learning environment outperformed those at the more traditional school, both on math problems requiring analytical or conceptual thought and on those requiring memory of a rule or formula. Three times as many students at the school emphasizing project-based learning received the top grade achievable on the national examination in math.

Many studies support the use of technology in project-based learning. For example, a study by the Center for Research in Educational Policy at the University of Memphis and University of Tennessee at Knoxville found that students using project-based learning and technology improved their test scores in all subject areas over a two-year period (Ross 2001).

However, one of the best-known studies of this kind was conducted by the Center for Children and Technology at the Education Development Center, Inc. A two-year technology trial that was implemented in Union City, New Jersey, in 1993 was monitored by the Center. The study found that after multimedia technology was used to support project-based learning, eighth graders scored 27 percentage points higher than students from other urban and special needs school districts on statewide tests in reading, math, and writing achievement. The study also found a decrease in absenteeism and an increase in students transferring to the school. Four years earlier, the state had been considering a takeover because Union City failed in 40 of 52 indicators of school effectiveness (Chang, et al. 1994).

The Importance of Assessment

Assessment is a critical piece in the project-based learning process. Teacher, students, and even parents may all take part in reviewing products based on established criteria. Students are typically assessed on several pieces of work (such as a portfolio) so that there is a varied representation of acquired skills and knowledge.

One of the most effective and useful assessment options is the rubric. A rubric lists a set of criteria that define and describe the important components of the work being planned or evaluated. A given criterion is then stated in several different levels of completion or competence, with a weighted score assigned to each level.

Rubrics are most effective when they are introduced at the beginning of a project. This way, students know what is expected of them and both the teacher and students can reference the rubric before, during, and after the project. This allows the rubric to be used as a planning tool, a monitoring tool, and an assessment tool. It is vitally important that the students see the rubric as a tool for themselves, and not just a way for the teacher to monitor their progress.

The Importance of Assessment (cont.)

Student checklists are another kind of assessment that may be used in project-based learning activities. The student checklist gives students the opportunity to check off required tasks or criteria they are to satisfy. Often, there will be several categories. For example, a checklist for a multimedia project might include categories such as organization, use of media, preparation, resources, appearance, and navigation. For each category, there is a list of tasks or criteria for the student to check off once completed or mastered. This allows students to monitor their own learning.

Another useful (and simple!) assessment tool in project-based learning is teacher observation. Teachers constantly observe and note what and how students are learning. This assessment puts a lot of emphasis on the process because observations may be conducted as students work on their projects rather than just evaluating the finished product. In addition, teachers may use checklists to track specific student behaviors or skills.

No matter what forms of assessment are used, it is important for assessment to take place throughout the duration of the project and not simply at the end once students have completed their work. The only way that students will know how they are doing and be able to monitor their own progress is by continuous feedback. The feedback will sometimes come from the teacher, but more often it may and should come from the students themselves. As the students reflect on and improve their work, they become actively engaged and responsible for their own learning. Also, because of the collaborative nature of project-based learning, students can become astute observers themselves and may be able to offer supportive and positive feedback to each other.

Table of Contents

Surveying Favorites

Activity Description

Students survey their classmates for information and create bar/column charts to display the data. Each student also writes one question that can be answered by looking at the chart.

Content Standard

Students understand that information can be represented in graphs.

Technology Skills

- starting a new workbook
- creating a bar/column chart
- entering text and numbers into cells
- saving and printing work

Materials

- chart paper and marker
- graphic organizer sheet for each student (p. 179; filename: *favsurv.pdf*)
- student sample (filename: *survey.xls*)

Teacher Preparation

1. Create a transparency of the student sample bar/column chart from the CD (filename: *survey.xls*) if you will be using an overhead projector. [Note: Bar and column charts are quite similar, so the two terms are used together in this lesson. However, *Excel* does distinguish between the two. The Procedure and Student Directions will lead students to create column charts.]

2. You may want students to work independently, in pairs, or in small groups. Review the procedure and consider various groupings before you begin to teach the lesson.

Procedure

Day One

1. Show students the bar/column sample chart from the CD (filename: *survey.xls*). Use the overhead or board.

2. Ask the students the following questions to get them thinking about this project.

   - *What is a survey?*
   - *What does a survey tell us?*
   - *What kind of information would you like to know about your classmates?*

3. Ask the students to consider different survey questions. Discuss how certain questions lend themselves to creating an *Excel* chart. Use a piece of chart paper to brainstorm a list of survey questions (e.g., eye color, number of siblings, number of pets, or favorite subject).

Procedure (*cont.*)

Day One (*cont.*)

4. Tell students that they will each decide on the topic for a survey.

5. Pass out the graphic organizer provided on page 179 (filename: *favsurv.pdf*).

6. Have the students decide on topics they want to survey and tell them to record their ideas on their graphic organizers. Continue to discuss the kinds of survey questions that lend themselves to creating charts.

7. Have the students draft their questions for the surveys. Give them an example or two if they need help.

8. Talk to the students about how they will conduct their surveys. Model for them how to fill in the categories and make tally marks as they get the survey information from their classmates. Let students suggest ways to complete this process.

9. Give students time to gather their data and tally their results.

Day Two

1. After the students finish tallying their data, show them how to sketch bar/column charts by hand on the graphic organizers.

2. After finishing their charts, talk to students about statements they can make based on the information in the charts. Have them record the statements on the graphic organizers.

3. Now, have students think of questions they can ask about their charts. Someone should be able to answer the question by looking at the chart. Have them record their questions on their graphic organizers.

Day Three

1. Explain to students they will now create bar/column charts using an *Excel* workbook. The Student Directions page shows steps that may work for your students as they complete their work at their computers.

2. Show the students how to open a new workbook (or spreadsheet file).

3. Show students how to type their survey categories across columns.

4. Show students how to type their survey results in the correct cells under the corresponding categories.

5. Model for the students how to select all the cells that contain data by clicking in the upper, left cell and dragging across to the lower, right cell.

6. Show the students how to create bar/column charts by clicking **Insert** on the Menu bar and clicking **_Chart_**. Or, have students click on the **Chart Wizard** button on the *Standard* toolbar.

Procedure (cont.)

Day Three (cont.)

7. In **Chart Wizard**, the bar/column chart will be the default choice. Leave everything as it is, and click on **Finish**. If your students have had experience with making charts in *Excel*, you might consider moving them through the **Chart Wizard** step by step to define the title and axes.

8. Show the students where and how to save their worksheets.

9. Have students print their charts by clicking on **File** in the Menu bar and choosing *Print*.

10. Give students sufficient time to complete the activity.

Day Four

1. Have a few of the students share their charts with the class and ask their questions.

2. Place students in pairs and have them ask one another their questions, using their charts to answer the questions.

3. Continue to give students new partners until each student has had the opportunity to ask at least three other students.

4. Use the rubric provided on page 181 to assess this lesson. There is also a blank rubric found on the Teacher Resource CD. You may want to have students help you create the rubric and be involved in the assessment of their projects.

Extension Ideas

Have students use the **Chart Options** menu to add axes labels and a title to the charts.

Allow students to create different types of charts for the same data (pie or line).

Surveying Favorites

The topic I decided to survey is _____.

The question I will ask is _____.

Categories					
Tally					

Before you use the computer to create a column chart of your data, sketch one below. Make sure to title your chart and label your axes.

Answer the questions below on a separate piece of paper.

- What is one statement you can make from looking at your column chart?
- What is one question you could ask that someone could answer by looking at your chart?

Surveying Favorites

Student Directions

1. Open a new workbook.

2. Type your first survey category in cell B2.

3. Type your next survey category in cell C2.

4. Continue typing your survey categories across row 2 until you have typed them all.

5. Starting with cell B3, type your first survey result.

6. Type your next survey result in cell C3.

7. Type the rest of your survey results across row 3.

8. Select all your cells. Click and hold on cell B2 and drag it to the last cell containing data in row 3.

9. Click **Insert** on the Menu bar. Choose **Chart**.

10. In the Chart Wizard dialog box, click on **Finish**.

11. Save your work.

12. Print your work.

Assessment Rubric

Strong **(3 Points)**	The student correctly typed in all the survey categories and the survey data.	All the survey data is correctly matched to the categories.	The student created a bar/column chart that reflects the survey data perfectly.	The student wrote a statement that describes a detailed, complex fact about the chart.	The student crafted a detailed, thoughtful question that requires higher-level thinking to answer.
Effective **(2 Points)**	The student typed in all the survey categories and the survey data with few errors.	Most of the survey data is matched to the categories.	The student created a bar/column chart that reflects the survey data.	The student wrote a statement that describes a fact about the chart.	The student crafted a question that can be answered by looking at the chart.
Emerging **(1 Point)**	The student typed in most of the survey categories and the survey data with few errors.	Some of the survey data is matched to the categories.	The student created a bar/column chart that somewhat reflects the survey data.	The student wrote a statement, but it inaccurately describes a fact about the chart.	The student crafted a question, but it is difficult to answer by simply looking at the chart.
Not Yet **(0 Points)**	The student typed in some of the survey categories and the survey data with errors.	The survey data does not match the categories.	The student created a bar/column chart, but it does not reflect the survey data.	The student wrote a statement, but it does not describe a fact about the chart.	The student crafted a question, but it cannot be answered by looking at the chart.
Self Score					
Teacher Score					
Total Score					
Comments:					

Lemonade Stand

Activity Description

Students use an example of a lemonade stand to decide on an object to sell and to compute how much to charge to make a profit.

Content Standard

Students determine reasonableness of a problem solution.

Technology Skills

- starting a new workbook
- entering text and numbers in to cells
- entering formulas
- formatting cells
- saving and printing work

Materials

- graphic organizer sheet for each student (p. 186; filename: lemstand.pdf)
- student sample (filename: *lemon.xls*)

Teacher Preparation

1. Print and review the student sample (filename: *lemon.xls*)

2. If necessary, review how to create formulas to perform calculations in *Microsoft Excel.*

3. You may want students to work independently, in pairs, or in small groups. Review the procedure and consider various groupings before you begin to teach the lesson.

Procedure

Day One

1. Ask students if they have ever sold lemonade or other goods to make money. Prompt a discussion with questions such as:

- *What did you sell?*
- *Where did you get your goods?*
- *Did you have to buy what you were selling?*
- *How much did you sell it for?*
- *How did you decide how much to sell it for?*
- *Did you sell it for more than it cost you?*

Procedure (cont.)

Day One (cont.)

2. Set up an imaginary scenario for the students. Tell them to imagine that they have paid $10 for 20 candy bars. Prompt a discussion with the following questions:

   - *How much did each candy bar cost you? How did you figure it out?*

   - *At what price would you have to sell the candy bars in order to make money?*

   - *How much do you think the price could be increased before people started buying fewer candy bars?*

3. Talk to the students about the balance of making a profit vs. charging so much for the candy bars that people would buy fewer or none at all.

4. Introduce the project to the students. Pass out copies of the graphic organizer provided on page 186 (filename: *lemstand.pdf*). Explain the scenario to the students.

5. Place the students into groups of two or three so they can work together to solve the problem.

6. Referring to the graphic organizer, tell students that they have enough lemonade mix to make 128 ounces of lemonade. This mix cost them $4.00. They also had to buy cups for $1.00.

7. Ask them how they would figure out how many 8-oz. cups of lemonade could be made from the mix (divide 128 by 8). Tell the students that when they solve the problem on their graphic organizers they will need to show their work and explain how they solved the problem.

8. Now, ask students how they would figure out how much to charge for a cup of lemonade. [Note: Because they can make 16 cups of lemonade, they multiply 16 by different numbers to see how much money they would get.] Explain to them that they need to make their $5 back and show a reasonable profit.

9. Remind students that the more they charge for a cup of lemonade, the fewer cups they might sell, but they have to charge enough to make a profit.

10. Allow the students to solve the problems on the graphic organizer in their groups. Remind them that they need to explain their solutions and show their work.

11. Monitor the students' work for accuracy and completeness as they work.

Procedure (*cont.*)

Day Two

1. Allow any students who have not finished the two problems on the graphic organizer to do so.

2. Explain to students they will now solve a similar problem in an *Excel* worksheet. Tell them they will be able to use an *Excel* worksheet to perform the calculations.

3. Show the students how to open a new *Microsoft Excel* workbook (or spreadsheet file) and type a title for the worksheet.

4. Ask students to consider what kind of item they would like to sell. [Note: You may want students to use the lemonade example to make the project a bit more accessible for students.] Decide what kind of sample you would like to share with students.

5. You may want to give students paper and pencils to use to write down ideas about their products. Students can work in pairs or in small groups.

6. Show students how to enter the two titles, *Ingredients* and *Cost*, in adjacent rows. Model for the students how to type the ingredients (such as lemonade mix and cups) in the cells in the *Ingredients* column and the dollar amounts in the cells in the *Cost* column. Do not include dollar signs, as you will later format the cells as currency.

7. Show the students how to widen the columns, if necessary, by clicking and dragging the column header boundary. Or, have students use the **Format** drop-down menu on the Menu bar. (See page 27.)

8. Title adjacent rows with appropriate headings describing other aspects of your chosen selling scenario.

9. Decide which formulas are necessary given your example. Point out the **Formula Bar** at the top of your screen. (If you cannot see it, you can click on **View** on the Menu bar and choose **Formula Bar**.) Explain that students can write formulas that will tell the computer how to compute numbers. Review the +, –, *, and / symbols and talk about how they are associated with addition, subtraction, multiplication, and division.

10. Review the use of cell labels (A1, A2, etc.). Write a simple addition formula. It might be as simple as =A1+A2. Tell students that formulas always start with an = sign.

11. Show students how to construct formulas that match the intent of the mathematical problem in your sample.

12. Show the students how to format the cells containing monetary values (including the ones with formulas) as currency. Click **Format** on the Menu bar, choose **Cells...** and click on the **Number** tab. Then, select *currency*.

Procedure (cont.)

Day Two (cont.)

13. Now, type different monetary values into the appropriate cells.

14. Show students where to save their worksheets and how to print them, if desired.

15. Give students sufficient time to complete the activity. You may decide to have them complete the work alone, in pairs, or in small groups. The Student Directions page shows steps that may work for your students as they complete their work at their computers.

Day Three

1. Review the reflection questions from the graphic organizer.

2. Give students time to complete that part of the graphic organizer.

3. Have student volunteers share their work with the class.

4. Have students give feedback to each student after their presentation.

5. Use the rubric provided on page 188 to assess this lesson. There is also a blank rubric found on the Teacher Resource CD. You may want to have students help you create the rubric and be involved in the assessment of their projects.

Extension Ideas

Have students use the SUM function instead of the addition formula to add a column.

Challenge the students to choose a different product to complete the project.

Lemonade Stand

Lemonade Stand Chart	
Ingredient	**Cost**
Lemonade mix for 128 ounces of drink	$4
Cups	$1
Total cost of ingredients	$5

How many 8-oz. cups of lemonade can you make from the mix provided? Explain how you figured it out. Show your work.

You paid $5 for the lemonade ingredients. How much will you have to charge for the cups of lemonade to break even? Explain how you figured it out. Show your work.

Reflect on the process of creating your lemonade stand by answering the following questions on a separate piece of paper.

- What was the hardest part of creating your lemonade stand?
- What formulas did you use in your worksheet? Be specific in your explanation.
- How much do you think you could charge without people thinking your product was too expensive?
- What do you think is the most important thing you learned from this project?

Lemonade Stand

Student Directions

1. Open a new *Excel* workbook.

2. Type a title in a cell in the first row.

3. Add titles to two adjacent rows such as *Ingredients* and *Cost*. Type the ingredients in the cells under *Ingredients* and the dollar amounts in the cells under *Cost*.

4. Widen the columns if necessary. Click and drag the column header boundary. Or, click **Format** on the Menu bar, choose **Column** and then *Width...*

5. Add other column or row headings.

6. Add your data.

7. What kind of formulas do you need? Use the **Formula Bar** at the top of your screen. (If you cannot see it, click **View** on the Menu bar and choose **Formula Bar**.)

8. Use the +, –, *, and / symbols. Remember that formulas always start with an equal sign (=).

9. Format the cells containing monetary values as currency. Click **Format** on the Menu bar, choose **Cells...**

10. Click on the **Number** tab and select *currency*.

11. Now, type different monetary values into the cells.

12. Save your work.

13. Print your work.

Assessment Rubric

Strong (3 Points)	The student independently formatted the worksheet correctly.	The cells containing dollar amounts are formatted as currency out to two decimal places, complete with a dollar sign.	The formulas are all correct.	The student's answers to the reflection questions are thorough and complete.	The student gives specific examples from the worksheet in answering the questions.
Effective (2 Points)	The student formatted the worksheet correctly with little support.	The cells containing dollar amounts are formatted as currency, but are not out to two decimal places or do not contain a dollar sign.	Some of the formulas are correct.	The student's answers to the reflection questions contain thought and detail.	The student gives some specific examples from the worksheet in answering the questions.
Emerging (1 Point)	The student formatted the worksheet somewhat correctly with some support.	The cells containing dollar amounts are formatted as currency, but are not out to two decimal places and do not contain a dollar sign.	A few of the formulas are correct.	The student's answers to the reflection questions could have contained more thought and detail.	The student gives a few general examples from the worksheet in answering the questions.
Not Yet (0 Points)	The student did not format the worksheet correctly.	The cells containing dollar amounts are not formatted as currency.	None of the formulas are correct.	The student's answers to the reflection questions do not show any reflection.	The student does not give examples from the worksheet in attempting to answer the questions.
Self Score					
Teacher Score					
Total Score					
Comments:					

Magic Squares

Activity Description

Students create a "magic square" using formulas to add the vertical, horizontal, and diagonal rows. Students then solve the magic squares to test the formulas.

Content Standard

Students use trial and error to solve problems.

Technology Skills

- starting a new worksheet
- entering text and numbers
- entering formulas
- formatting cells
- adding borders to cells
- saving and printing work

Materials

- graphic organizer sheets for students (p. 193; filename: *magsqr.pdf*)
- student sample (filename: *magic.xls*)

Teacher Preparation

1. Print and review the student sample (filename: *magic.xls*)

2. If necessary, review for yourself how to create formulas to perform calculations in *Excel*.

3. If desired, obtain additional examples of magic squares from the Internet. A simple search using the key words *magic square example* should yield many examples you can print out.

Procedure

Day One

1. Show the following magic square to students. You may put it on the overhead or board.

6	1	8
7	5	3
2	9	4

2. Ask the students what they notice about the magic square. Possible responses might include:

- The squares contain the numbers 1–9.
- No numbers are repeated.
- The numbers in any row, column, or diagonal add to 15.
- The number in the middle is used in four addition problems (6+5+4; 8+5+2; 7+5+3; 1+5+9).
- The numbers on the corners of the square are used in three addition problems.
- The numbers in the middle edges of the square are used in two addition problems.

Procedure (*cont.*)

Day One (*cont.*)

3. Explain the concept of a magic square to the students. There are nine numbers in a magic square. Numbers may only be used once, and only once. Each row, column, and diagonal add up to the same number. Tell students there are many other number combinations that can be used to make magic squares. In the example provided on page 189, numbers 1–9 added to 15.

4. Introduce the project to the students. Pass out copies of the graphic organizer to the students. Place the students into groups of two or three so they can work together to solve the problem.

5. Referring to the graphic organizer, tell the students they have to solve magic squares using the numbers 1–9, with each column, row, and diagonal adding to 12.

6. Model guessing and checking for the students, and don't focus yet on the hint given in the graphic organizer. [Note: Some students may notice the hint and use it. This is fine.]

7. Allow the students to work in their groups to begin solving the magic squares. Let them work for 10 minutes or so before explaining the hint.

8. Explain the hint that is given on the graphic organizer. Have the students make a list of all eight possible equations with three addends that add up to 12. The number that occurs four times in the list will be the center number (since the center number is involved in four equations in the magic square.) By the same token, all corner numbers will occur three times in the list, and the middle edge numbers will occur two times in the list. When students grasp this concept, the puzzle becomes much easier to solve. The challenge is coming up with eight correct equations.

9. Allow the students to continue working on their magic squares.

10. Students who solve the magic square early can be given additional magic square combinations to solve.

    - the numbers 2–10 with a sum of 18
    - the numbers 3–11 with a sum of 21
    - the numbers 4–12 with a sum of 24
    - the numbers 5–13 with a sum of 27

11. Monitor the students' work for accuracy and completeness.

Procedure (*cont.*)

Day Two

1. Allow any students who haven't finished the magic square on the graphic organizer to do so.

2. Explain to students they will now put magic squares into worksheets. Tell them they will be able to use the worksheets to perform the calculations.

3. Show the students how to open a new worksheet and type a title.

4. Show students how to select rows by clicking and dragging across the row headings for rows 3, 4, 5, and 6.

5. Model changing the row height by clicking **Format** on the Menu bar. Choose **Row** and then *Height...* Set the height at 1 in./96 pixels.

6. Select cells B3 through D5 by clicking, holding, and dragging across them.

7. Show the students how to create a border around the selected cells by clicking on the **Borders** button on the *Formatting* toolbar to create an outside border for these nine cells.

8. Now, show the students how to create formulas that will add each row, column, and diagonal. In cell E3, type a formula that adds the contents of cells B3, C3, and D3 (=B3+C3+D3).

9. Continue showing the students how to create formulas that add the rows, columns, and diagonals in the magic square.

10. Now, demonstrate how the workbook application calculates the sum of the three cells in the rows, diagonals, and columns when numbers are typed into the cells of the magic square.

11. Tell the students they will be creating their own magic square worksheets, and will solve them for at least two of the following combinations:

    - the numbers 2–10 with a sum of 18
    - the numbers 3–11 with a sum of 21
    - the numbers 4–12 with a sum of 24
    - the numbers 5–13 with a sum of 27

12. Show students where to save their worksheets.

13. Have students print their worksheets.

14. Give students sufficient time to complete the activity. You may decide to have them work alone, in pairs, or in small groups. The Student Directions page shows steps that may work for your students as they complete their work at the computer.

Procedure *(cont.)*

Day Three

1. Tell student volunteers that they will present their own squares to the class. Talk about how to make an effective oral presentation to others.

2. Have students work in teams to solve the squares.

3. Have students give feedback to each student after the presentation.

4. Use the rubric provided on page 195 to assess this lesson. There is also a blank rubric found on the Teacher Resource CD. You may want students to help you create the rubric and be involved in the assessment of their projects.

Extension Ideas

Have students use the AutoSum feature to add the columns, rows, and diagonals instead of the addition formula.

Challenge the students to solve a 4 x 4 magic square, using the numbers 1–16 with each row, column, and diagonal adding to 34.

Magic Squares

What is a magic square? All magic squares with three rows and three columns have the following attributes in common:

1. There are nine numbers.

2. Each number is used only once.

3. Each row, column, and diagonal adds to the same number.

This magic square contains the numbers 1–9 and each row, column, and diagonal adds to 15. Notice that each number is used only once.

6	1	8	15
7	5	3	15
2	9	4	15
15	15	15	15

There are many other number combinations that you can use to create a magic square. Below is a magic square for you to solve.

Directions: Use the numbers 1–9 in the magic square below so that each column, row, and diagonal adds to 12.

When you create your own magic square in the worksheet, you will be choosing from the following combinations:

Hint: List the eight ways you can make 12 using three addends. Find the number that occurs four times in the eight ways, and that number will be in the center of the magic square. Think of the corner numbers. How many times in the eight ways will the corner numbers occur? What about the middle edge numbers?

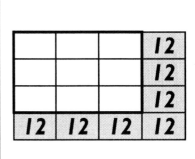

- the numbers 2–10 with a sum of 18

- the numbers 3–11 with a sum of 21

- the numbers 4–12 with a sum of 24

- the numbers 5–13 with a sum of 27

Reflect on the process of creating a magic square by answering the following questions on a separate piece of paper.

- What was the hardest part of creating your magic square in the worksheet?

- What formulas did you use in your worksheet? Be specific in your explanation.

- How did you solve the magic square? Did you use guess and check or another method?

- What do you think is the most important thing you learned from this project?

Magic Squares

Student Directions

1. Open a new workbook.

2. Type a title in a cell in the first row.

3. Select rows 3, 4, 5, and 6 by clicking and dragging across the row headings for rows 3, 4, 5, and 6. Click **Format** on the Menu bar. Choose **Row** and then *Height...* Change the row height to 1 in./96 pixels. This will make the cells square-shaped.

4. Select cells B3 through D5 by clicking, holding, and dragging across them.

5. Find the *Formatting* toolbar. Click **View** on the Menu bar. Click **Toolbars>** and choose *Formatting*.

6. Create a border around the selected cells. Click the **Borders** button on the *Formatting* toolbar to create an outside border for these nine cells.

7. Create formulas that will add each row, column, and diagonal.

8. Start with cell E3. In cell E3, type a formula that adds the contents of cells B3, C3, and D3.

9. Continue creating formulas that add the rows, columns, and diagonals in the magic square.

10. Test your formulas by typing numbers in the cells of the magic square and notice if the sums that display in the cells containing the formulas are correct.

11. Solve your magic square for at least two of the following combinations:

    - the numbers 2–10 with a sum of 18
    - the numbers 3–11 with a sum of 21
    - the numbers 4–12 with a sum of 24
    - the numbers 5–13 with a sum of 27

12. Save your work.

Assessment Rubric

Strong (3 Points)	The student formatted the entire worksheet correctly.	The cells containing the magic square are square in shape and proper borders have been applied around the 3 x 3 cell matrix.	The eight formulas for adding the rows, columns, and diagonals are all correct.	All of the student's answers to the reflection questions are thorough and complete.
Effective (2 Points)	The student formatted most of the worksheet correctly.	The cells containing the magic square are mostly square in shape and borders have been applied around the 3 x 3 cell matrix.	At least seven of the formulas for adding the rows, columns, and diagonals are correct.	Most of the student's answers to the reflection questions are thorough and complete.
Emerging (1 Point)	The student formatted some of worksheet correctly.	The cells containing the magic square are square in shape, but proper borders have not been applied around the 3 x 3 cell matrix.	Fewer than six of the formulas for adding the rows, columns, and diagonals are correct.	Few of the student's answers to the reflection questions are thorough and complete.
Not Yet (0 Points)	The student did not format the worksheet correctly.	The cells containing the magic square are not square in shape and the proper borders have not been applied around the 3 x 3 cell matrix.	Fewer than four of the formulas for adding the rows, columns, and diagonals are correct.	The student's answers to the reflection questions show no reflection.
Self Score				
Teacher Score				
Total Score				
Comments:				

Your Monthly Budget

Activity Description

Students design monthly budgets. They include formulas to help calculate their budgets.

Content Standard

Students use computers for computation.

Technology Skills

- starting a new workbook
- entering text and numbers
- entering formulas
- formatting cells
- saving and printing work

Materials

- newspaper advertisements for food and other consumer goods
- graphic organizer sheets for students (p. 200; filename: *mbudget.pdf*)
- student sample (filename: *budget.xls*)

Teacher Preparation

1. Print and review the student sample (filename: *budget.xls*)

2. Prepare materials and advertisements for students to get prices for their monthly budgets. You may use newspaper ads or find information online.

3. If necessary, review how to create formulas to perform calculations in *Microsoft Excel*.

4. This lesson procedure is written to teach students how to budget a $1,500 monthly "salary." You may want to change the amount depending on the economic and social situations in your students' lives.

Procedure

Day One

1. Ask students the following questions to get them thinking about how much money it takes to live for a month.

   - Imagine you have moved out of your parent's house. You are now responsible for all your expenses. What types of expenses would you have? [Note: Students will probably not think about expenses such as taxes and insurance.]

   - Imagine you have $1,500 to spend per month. How much money do you think the government would take in taxes before you get your share? [Note: You can set a percentage amount, such as 20%, that goes to taxes.]

Procedure (cont.)

Day One (cont.)

- How much do you think it costs per month to rent an apartment?

- How much do you think it costs for car insurance per month for someone under 25?

2. Explain to students they will pretend to have a $1,500 to spend to live for one month. They will create monthly budgets that do not exceed their monthly intake.

3. Brainstorm a list of things that need to be included in the monthly budget. At a minimum, the students should include the following:

  - rent and utilities (gas, electric, water, trash)

  - car payment and insurance

  - food

  - entertainment

  - savings account

4. Have a discussion about wants vs. needs. For example, is a cell phone absolutely necessary? What about a car?

5. Model for the students how to use the resources you have chosen (newspaper ads or websites) to get figures for their budgets. Talk to the students about some of the decisions they will have to make (e.g., how nice a car to buy; how big an apartment to rent, etc.).

6. Show the students how to fill in the graphic organizer on page 200 (filename: *mbudget.pdf*).

7. Place students into groups of three or four. Have the students work together to research the figures for their monthly budgets and begin filling out the graphic organizers. Make sure they calculate their monthly salaries.

8. Remind students to keep an eye on their monthly totals and adjust their spending if necessary. They might have to rent a smaller apartment or buy a cheaper car!

Day Two

1. Have students continue researching their monthly budgets and filling out their graphic organizers.

2. Monitor the students' work for accuracy and completeness as they continue.

Day Three

1. Explain to students they will now enter their monthly budgets into worksheets. Tell them they will be able to use the worksheets to perform many of their budgetary calculations.

2. Show students how to open new worksheets and type a title for their worksheets.

Procedure (cont.)

Day Three (cont.)

3. Model for the students how to type the budget categories (e.g., rent, car payment, etc.) in the cells of one column and the dollar amounts in the adjacent column. Do not type dollar signs because you will later show students how to format the cells as currency. Make sure to include a category for a savings account.

4. Show the students how to widen the columns if necessary by clicking and dragging the column header boundary.

5. Type headings for *My Monthly Budget*, *Total*, and *$1,500* in cells A1, A2, and B2. See the student sample provided (filename: *budget.xls*).

6. In the cell next to the *Salary After Taxes* heading, type a formula that multiplies the contents of the cell containing the gross salary by 80%. For example, if the gross salary is in cell B2, the formula would be (=B2*0.8), without the parentheses. This will give the after taxes monthly salary.

7. Highlight or bold the *Salary After Taxes* row.

8. In the cell below the last budget category dollar amount, type a formula that calculates the sum of the cells above it. For example, if the budget category dollar amounts are in cells B6 through B14, the formula would be (=B6+B7+B8+B9+B10+B11+B12+B13+B14).

9. Show the students how to format the cells containing monetary values (including the ones with formulas) as currency. Click **Format** on the Menu bar, choose **Cells...** Click on the **Number** tab, and then select *currency*.

10. You can now compare the monthly salary to the total of the bills. If the monthly salary is less than the bills, explain to the students that they will have to adjust their spending. You could have the students create a formula in a cell subtracting the monthly bills from the monthly salary so this calculation is performed automatically.

11. Show the students where to save their worksheets. Model printing the worksheet, if desired.

12. Give students sufficient time to complete the activity. You may decide to have them work alone, in pairs, or in small groups. The Student Directions page shows steps that may work for your students as they complete their work at their computers.

Procedure *(cont.)*

Day Four

1. Review the reflection questions from the graphic organizer on page 200 (filename: *mbudget.pdf*).

2. Give students time to complete that part of their graphic organizers.

3. Have student volunteers share their work with the class.

4. Have students give feedback to each student after the presentation.

5. Use the rubric provided on page 202 to assess this lesson. There is also a blank rubric found on the Teacher Resource CD. You may want students to help you create the rubric and be involved in the assessment of their projects.

Extension Ideas

Have students use the AutoSum function to add the category column instead of the addition formula.

Have the students research salaries of various occupations with and without college degrees for comparison.

Name _____

Your Monthly Budget

Your Monthly Budget	
Monthly Salary (gross)	**Salary After Taxes**
$1,500	
Expense	**Cost**
Rent	

Reflect on the process of creating your monthly budget by answering the following questions:

● What was the hardest part of creating your monthly budget? _____

● Did your monthly salary go faster than you thought? _____

● Were there things you wanted to include in your monthly budget but could not? If so, what were they?

_____

● What do you think is the most important thing you learned from this project? _____

_____

Your Monthly Budget

Student Directions

1. Open a new workbook.

2. Type the budget categories (*rent, car payment*, etc.) in the cells of one column. Type the dollar amounts in the adjacent column.

3. Widen the columns if necessary by clicking and dragging the column header boundary.

4. Title your headings: *My Monthly Budget, Total,* and *$1,500.*

5. Type your subheading: *Salary After Taxes.*

6. In the cell next to *Salary After Taxes,* type a formula that multiplies the contents of the cell containing the gross salary by 80%. For example, if the gross salary is in cell B2, the formula would be (=B2*0.8), without the parentheses. This will give the after-taxes monthly salary. This is called your *net salary.*

7. Find the *Formatting* toolbar. Click **View** on the Menu bar. Click **Toolbars>** and choose *Formatting.* Use this toolbar to Bold or add a fill color to the *Salary After Taxes* row.

8. In the cell below the last budget category dollar amount, type a formula that calculates the sum of the cells above it. For example, if the budget category dollar amounts are in cells B6 through B14, the formula would be (=B6+B7+B8+B9+B10+B11+B12+B13+B14).

9. Format the cells containing monetary values (including the ones with formulas) as currency. Click **Format** on the Menu bar, choose **Cells...** Click on the *Number* tab and then select *currency.*

10. You can now compare the monthly salary to the total of the bills. Can you create a cell with a formula that calculates the difference between these two amounts? If the monthly salary is less than the bills, you will have to adjust your spending. Perhaps you will have to spend less on your apartment, or use public transportation instead of a car.

11. Save your work.

Strong **(3 Points)**	The student chose realistic categories for the budget. The categories reflect a real-life scenario, and cover all major expenses he or she would encounter.	The student formatted the entire worksheet correctly.	All of the formulas in the worksheet are correct.	The student presented a realistic monthly budget and spent less than the monthly salary.
Effective **(2 Points)**	The student mostly chose realistic categories for the budget. The categories reflect a real-life scenario, and cover nearly all major expenses he or she would encounter.	The student formatted most of the worksheet correctly.	Some of the formulas in the worksheet are correct.	The student presented somewhat of a realistic monthly budget and spent less than the monthly salary.
Emerging **(1 Point)**	The student did not choose realistic categories for the budget. The categories somewhat reflect a real-life scenario, and cover some of the major expenses he or she would encounter.	The student formatted some of the worksheet correctly.	Few of the formulas in the worksheet are correct.	The student presented a monthly budget, but did not spend less than the monthly salary.
Not Yet **(0 Points)**	The student chose unrealistic categories for the budget. The categories do not reflect a real-life scenario and cover few of the major expenses he or she would encounter.	The student did not format the worksheet correctly.	None of the formulas in the worksheet are correct.	The student presented an unrealistic monthly budget and did not spend less than the monthly salary.
Self Score				
Teacher Score				
Total Score				
Comments:				

Table of Contents

Works Cited

Boaler, Jo. 1999. Mathematics for the moment or the millennium? *Education Week* 29:30, 34.

Britt, Judy, Joe P. Brasher, Lydia D. Davenport. 2007. Balancing books & bytes. *Kappa Delta Pi*, 43: 122–127.

Chang, Han-hua, Margaret Honey, Daniel Light, Babette Moeller, and Nancy Ross. 1994. *The Union City story: Education reform and technology students' performance on standardized tests.* Education Development Center.

Eisenberg, Michael B., and Doug Johnson. 1996. Computer skills for information problem solving: Learning and teaching technology in context. *Emergency Librarian.*

Mitchell, Karen, Marianne Bakia, and Edith Yang. 2007. State strategies and practices for educational technology: Volume II—Supporting mathematics instruction with educational technology. Washington, DC: U.S. Department of Education, Office of Planning, Evaluation, and Policy Development.

Moursund, David. 1999. *Project based learning: Using information technology.* Eugene, OR: International Society for Technology in Education.

Ross, Steven. The Center for Research in Educational Policy. http://crep.memphis.edu/web/research.

Stites, Regie. 1998. Evaluation of project-based learning: What does research say about outcomes from project-based learning? The Challenge 2000 Multimedia Project. http://pblmm.k12.ca.us/PBLGuide/pblresch.htm (accessed 3/20/07).

TeacherVision. 2007. Learner-centered vs. curriculum-centered teachers: Which one are you? http://www.teachervision.fen.com/teaching-methods/curriculum-planning/4786.html (accessed 1/14/07).

Valdez, Gilbert, Mary McNabb, May Foertsch, May Anderson, Mark Hawkdes, and Lenaya Raack. 1999. Computer-based technology and learning: Evolving uses and expectations. North Central Regional Educational Laboratory.

White, Noel, Cathy Ringstaff, and Loretta Kelley. 2002. *Getting the most from technology in schools.* San Francisco, CA: WestEd.

Other References

4Teachers. Project based learning checklists. http://pblchecklist.4teachers.org/checklist.shtml (accessed 5/14/07).

The George Lucas Educational Foundation. Why is problem-based learning important? http://www.edutopia.org/modules/PBL/whypbl.php (accessed 1/14/07).

Content-Area Index

Teacher Resource CD Index

Sample Student Projects

Page	Lesson Title	Filename
15	Number Fun	fun.xls
19	Symmetry Design	symm.xls
23	Mystery Fill Designs	myst.xls
28	Spelling Fun	spell.xls
32	Guess the Word	guess.xls
36	Crossword Puzzle	cross.xls
41	Favorite Animal	anim.xls
45	Cloud Information Chart	cloud.xls
49	Planet Comparison Chart	planet.xls
54	Reading List	list.xls
58	Book List	book.xls
62	Literature Record	lit.xls
67	Favorite Ice Cream Survey	ice.xls
71	Favorite Pizza Survey	pizza.xls
75	Favorite Elective Survey	elect.xls
80	Favorite Ice Cream Chart	chart.xls
84	Favorite Pizza Chart	favtop.xls
88	Favorite Elective Chart	favelect.xls
93	Helper Reward Chart	helper.xls
97	Weekend Schedule	wkend.xls
101	Income and Expense Chart	expense.xls
106	Spelling Test Record	test.xls
110	Temperature Averages Record	temp.xls
114	Stock Prices Record	stock.xls
119	Shoe Choice Chart	shoe.xls
123	Recess Activity Chart	recess.xls
127	Food Nutrition Chart	cal.xls
132	Beginning Word Problems	calc.xls
136	Intermediate Word Problems	word.xls
140	Advanced Word Problems	advan.xls
145	Dinosaur Facts	dino.xls
149	Roller Coaster Facts	roller.xls
153	Country Comparisons	country.xls
158	Family Celebrations	family.xls
162	City Population Statistics	city.xls
166	Persuading an Audience	pers.xls
176	Surveying Favorites	survey.xls
182	Lemonade Stand	lemon.xls
189	Magic Squares	magic.xls
196	Your Monthly Budget	budget.xls
varies	Blank Rubric	rubric.doc

Teacher Resource CD Index *(cont.)*

Macintosh Screenshots of Summary Pages

Page	Lesson	Filename
14	Getting Started	start.pdf
27	Formatting Cells	cells.pdf
40	Changing Rows and Columns	rows.pdf
53	Sorting Lists	lists.pdf
66	Creating a Data Table	table.pdf
79	Creating a Chart	chart.pdf
92	Working with Numbers	numbers.pdf
105	Creating a Line Chart	linechrt.pdf
118	Creating a Pie Chart	piechrt.pdf
131	Using Functions and Formulas	function.pdf
144	Displaying and Printing	printing.pdf
157	Special Features	special.pdf

Graphic Organizers/Data Collection Grids

Page	Lesson	Filename
176	Surveying Favorites	favsurv.pdf
182	Lemonade Stand	lemstand.pdf
189	Magic Squares	magsqr.pdf
196	Your Monthly Budget	mbudget.pdf

Learn & Use Series Description

Inspiration Skills Covered

* Adding a Symbol to a Diagram
* Using the Symbol Palette
* Adding and Formatting Text to a Diagram
* Formatting Symbols
* Adding, Deleting, and Changing Direction of Links
* Using the Draw Tools
* Using the Arrange Tool
* Grouping and Ungrouping Symbols and Objects
* Switching Between Diagram View and Outline View
* Adding and Moving Topics and Subtopics in an Outline
* Showing, Hiding, and Changing Prefixes in an Outline
* Using Notes
* Using the Word Guide
* Inserting a Hyperlink
* Using the Checklist Tool
* Recording Sound
* Learning Printing Options
* Transferring Work to a Word Processor

Microsoft Word Skills Covered

* Inserting, Deleting, Moving Text
* Changing Text Appearance
* Formatting a Document
* Printing a Document
* Using Shapes and Lines
* Inserting and Formatting a Table
* Using Clip Art
* Using Spelling Check, Grammar Check, and Thesaurus
* Inserting Images
* WordArt
* Using Columns
* Using Wizards and Templates

Kidspiration Skills Covered

* Using a Learning Activity
* Finding Symbol Libraries
* Adding a Symbol to a Diagram
* Formatting Symbols
* Adding Text to Symbols
* Copying, Pasting, and Deleting Symbols
* Formatting Text
* Copying and Pasting Text
* Adding Text in Writing View
* Formatting Text in Writing View
* Linking Symbols
* Formatting Lines and Arrows
* Adding Text to a Link
* Using the Listen Tool
* Using a SuperGrouper Category
* Adding Symbols to a SuperGrouper Category
* Importing a Graphic
* Recording Sound

Microsoft PowerPoint Skills Covered

* Inserting, Deleting, and Moving a Text Box
* Changing Text Appearance
* Adding a Picture or Clip Art
* Changing Borders and Backgrounds
* Putting Slides in Order
* Playing a Slide Show
* Inserting and Formatting a Table or Chart
* Using Slide Transitions
* Animating a Picture or Text
* Using Online and Animated Clips
* Including Audio
* Using Hyperlinks